Praise for *Eyes Up!*

"TJ Kostecky has done us all a favor with his delightful book *Eyes Up!*, in which he shares simple yet profound ways to experience the world and its possibilities anew. With vivid storytelling and infectious positivity, TJ easily convinces the reader that his recommendations are immediately doable in many facets of our lives and that they can bring instant change to how we perceive our own potential. I found great advice here for improving my own decision-making. As an added plus, TJ's book made me appreciate soccer, a sport I have long enjoyed, in a new light. Reading this book is like getting great advice about life from a supportive, enthusiastic, wise, and humble friend."

—Malia Du Mont, Chief of Staff & VP for Strategy & Policy,
Bard College, NY, and former Strategist, Office of the Secretary of Defense

"With *Eyes Up!*, TJ Kostecky shares his vivid personal account of a life enriched by his Vision Training soccer program and the transformational leadership workshops that have evolved out of it. TJ has traveled the world espousing a life of 'look, listen, learn' and formed a grateful appreciation for what makes each of us unique—at a time when community and connectivity are needed most. A most inspiring read indeed!"

—Joseph A. Machnik, PhD, World Cup TV Soccer Rules Analyst,
National Soccer Hall of Fame

"*Eyes Up!* provides an inspiring road map to expand your perspective and deepen your impact on the people and community around you. Drawing on personal stories from decades of player-centric coaching, TJ shares tangible practices that all leaders can apply on the field and in life."

—Michael R. Minogue, President and CEO, Minogue Consulting LLC;
Chairman, Michael and Renee Minogue Foundation;
and retired Chairman, President and CEO Abiomed, Inc.

"*Eyes Up!* is a highly relevant, thoroughly enjoyable read for people of both sporting and non-sporting backgrounds. TJ weaves his strong personal values through fact-based leadership strategies aimed at improving one's perspective and experiences. He succinctly links his Vision Training methodology in soccer with his own personal connections and stories to animate and activate the Vision Training for Life program, making it accessible to readers from all walks of life."

—Adam Janssen, High Performance Director,
Canadian Paralympic Committee, and former Goalkeeper,
Canadian Olympic Team

"Coach TJ weaves his personal philosophy, psychology, and insights about the 'beautiful game' to help readers appreciate connections throughout their lives, both on and off the field. From his lifelong career as a successful soccer coach, Coach TJ shares anecdotes filled with charm and wisdom. He challenges us to see the world with fresh eyes and shows us how to find deeper meaning and purpose in the everyday."

—Tracy Trevorrow, Professor of Psychology & Director,
Center for Medical Psychology, Chaminade University, HI,
and Author, *The Fourth Foundation*

"*Eyes Up!* delivers real-life tools for success whether you're a coach, student-athlete, parent, or corner-office executive. It's a book full of thoughtful lessons to inspire us in our daily decisions, to make the world a better place, and to become kinder, happier people along the way. TJ combines sport and life encounters to show us ways to broaden our lens and create a life-solution road map with positive outcomes, no matter the challenges or obstacles before us. His experiences create a clear window into what it means to lead an 'eyes up' life, using the 5 Ps and 3 Ls as guiding forces. By following TJ's teachings, you will become not just

a better player/coach/leader; you will become a better person. *Eyes Up!* is a book that provides substance, insight, and the foundation for living your best life."
—Terry Wansart, Director of Athletics, Hunter College, NY

"TJ distills lessons and concepts from his experiences of interacting and connecting with others and brings them to life in the most compelling manner. The lessons emphasize that growing our values and priorities involves a broad range of positive interactions with others. We never know when the most routine and ordinary encounters will bring true insight and meaning."
—Dave Simeone, Director of Education Programs,
United Soccer Coaches of America

"*Eyes Up!* is a book about soccer and how to play the beautiful game. But it is so much more. It is philosophy, anthropology, memoir, advice, metaphysics, physiology, ethics, and psychology. As a former Division I athlete, I am struck by how deeply the core of TJ's book embodies compassion and generosity. Yes, TJ's teaching will lead to more wins on the playing field. But more than that, it will stimulate thoughtful, considerate, energized, perceptive, engaged human experience. TJ has demonstrated—with fascinating and wide-ranging stories about coaching, family, work, and relationships—how meaning, connection, and purpose bring us into the fullness of life."
—Paul Marienthal, Dean for Social Action and Director of the
Trustee Leader Scholar Program, Bard College, NY,
and former Captain, Stanford University Men's Tennis

EYES UP!

EYES UP!

Discover Your Full Potential
and Form Meaningful Connections
Through Subtle Shifts in Perspective

TJ Kostecky
with Dan DiClerico

Matt Holt Books
An Imprint of BenBella Books, Inc.
Dallas, TX

Matt Holt is an imprint of BenBella Books, Inc.

10440 N. Central Expressway
Suite 800
Dallas, TX 75231
benbellabooks.com
Send feedback to feedback@benbellabooks.com

BenBella and *Matt Holt* are federally registered trademarks.

Printed in the United States of America
10 9 8 7 6 5 4 3 2 1

Library of Congress Control Number: 2023030381
ISBN 9781637744666 (hardcover)
ISBN 9781637744673 (electronic)

Editing by Katie Dickman
Copyediting by Michael Fedison
Proofreading by Christine Florie and Cape Cod Compositors, Inc.
Text design and composition by Jordan Koluch
Cover design by Brigid Pearson
Vision Training for Life logo courtesy of Beth Sillen
Printed by Lake Book Manufacturing

To Kate and Caroline,
your kindness, curiosity, and spirit inspire us all.

Contents

PART III: FINDING THE GOOD IN OTHERS

INTRODUCTION

Synchronicity is an ever present reality
for those who have eyes to see it.
Carl Jung

One of the greatest goals in U.S. soccer history came fifteen minutes into the 2015 FIFA Women's World Cup final against Japan. Carli Lloyd, Team USA's wily, veteran captain, collected a loose ball near the midfield line and, after a few deft touches, sent it soaring fifty yards into the back of Japan's net. While the strike itself was a dazzling display of talent, the goal only happened because of something Lloyd did a split second earlier. She lifted her **eyes up**.

With that slight, barely perceptible shift in perspective, Lloyd managed to scan the field around her, collecting data points that other players missed—the angle of the defense, the proximity of her teammates, and, most importantly, the fact that Japan's keeper was dangerously adrift from her own goal line. Lloyd saw her chance and took it, and with the conversion, cemented her place in the firmament of U.S. soccer legends.

I was some three thousand miles away at the time, watching the World Cup from my apartment in Brooklyn, near the campus of Long Island University, where I ran the school's Division I men's soccer program from 1999 to 2019. I immediately spotted the quick lift of the head that led to Lloyd's goal, and it gave me a small measure of pride. Though I never trained Carli directly, her college coach was a big adopter of Vision Training, the soccer program that I co-created with Len Bilous in 1981 to empower players to make smart decisions by expanding their field of vision.

Over the decades, Vision Training has helped tens of thousands of U.S. players, including luminaries like Lloyd, Claudio Reyna, and Julie Foudy, plus countless youth, high school, and college athletes. The program has also been embraced internationally, by clubs at every level in countries like Costa Rica, Canada, Finland, and Ukraine, to name just a few.

In recent years, I've taken my teachings beyond the soccer field, with leadership workshops that start with the basics of Vision Training, then layer on additional ideals and principles, like integrity, purpose, and the power of synchronicity. It's all about living every day with your **eyes up**, recognizing new and unique opportunities and having the wherewithal to seize on them, just like those players on the field who see and do things that others miss. To make that point more clearly, let me ask you a few questions:

- Do you wish you could form deeper and more meaningful connections within your community, if only you could figure out the right way in?
- Do you want to find ways to become a purposeful and more transformative leader?
- Are you often paralyzed by major life decisions, including those related to your career and family, because you're unable to think through the different outcomes?
- Have you ever missed out on the chance to get to know someone better, maybe a colleague or fellow volunteer, simply because you couldn't remember their name?

If you answered "yes" to any of these questions, your lens may not be as wide, deep, and bright as it could be. I truly believe the lessons contained in this book will help and, in the process, change your life for the better. I am so excited to show you how small shifts in perspective can have a major impact on how you see the world and live your life, leading to higher levels of success and satisfaction. These benefits won't just be for you, but also for every other person in your orbit. Carli Lloyd might have gotten the hat trick that day in the USA's 5–2 defeat of Japan, a feat that helped earn her the Golden Ball as the tournament's top player. But when the moment came to raise the 2015 World Cup trophy, she was standing shoulder-to-shoulder with her twenty-two teammates, plus the entire nation back home that was elevated by her greatness.

This is the wonderfully transformative power of Vision Training, its ability to improve your life *and* make the world a better place. It might sound like magic, especially since the results are often so immediate. In fact, it's simply about applying the process I've re-fined over decades to expand your lens and take in more of what the universe has to offer. Now, what do you say we get started? Let's go—**eyes up**!

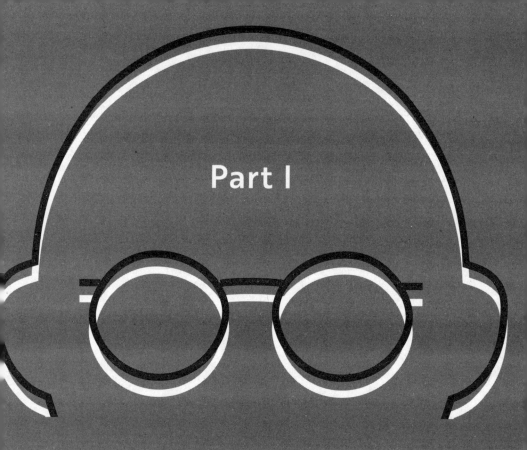

Part I

CHANGE YOUR LENS, CHANGE YOUR LIFE

Chapter One

THE POWER OF PERCEPTION

When I was twelve years old, a run-in with an old, rusty nail changed the way I saw the world forever. It was 1971 in the small town of Fords, New Jersey, where I lived with my parents, Antonin (Tony) and Ludmilla (Lucy), and my older sister, Nina. Ukrainian refugees of World War II, my folks were hardworking immigrants who had chosen to raise a family in this quiet, middle-class community near the Jersey shore, over the hustle of the big city.

They were both educated, my father in medicine, and he enjoyed his work as a cytologist, studying human cancer cells. Mom started off as a bank teller and eventually became a manager at the local branch. And I was your typical child of the late '60s, early '70s. This was before video games and cable TV, so there was a lot of riding bikes, playing games, and exploring the woods behind Fords Junior High School. I never got into any serious trouble—a "good boy" is how my mother and sister used to describe me—but I was always up for adventure.

My best friend at the time, Donnie Carrington, was the courageous and mischievous one. That's how we wound up in the forest that early summer afternoon. Growing up, I always spent the bulk of my summer break at a Ukrainian camp in the Catskills. But this was in the window between when school let out and camp started.

"Come on, TJ, let's go to the woods," Donnie said, jumping on his ten-speed.

"Okay, sure!" I answered, pedaling eagerly to catch up to him.

We dropped our bikes at the edge of the grass field and ventured into the forest. About fifty yards in we came upon the perfect climbing tree, a towering birch with a beautiful round bough. The only problem was the trunk was as slick as oil and the lowest branches were too high to reach.

"We need to build a ladder," Donnie said. His dad was an electrician, so besides being adventurous, he was handy. We biked back to his house and grabbed a few tools and scraps of lumber. Back at the tree, Donnie positioned the first step about chest high and lined up the nail. I was standing directly behind him, a few steps back so as not to get whacked by the backswing of the hammer. I never considered the possibility that the nail would break off, fly through the air, and plunge into my eye. That's exactly what happened. I fell to the ground in a heap.

"Holy crap, TJ, are you okay?" Donnie cried.

I pulled my hand away from my eye and tried to open it.

"I can't see, Donnie!" I screamed. I jumped on my bike and high-tailed it back home. Thankfully it was a Saturday, so my mom was there. I flew into the kitchen and told her what had happened, still clutching my right eye. She laid me down on the living room couch and placed a damp cloth over the wound. Between her soothing tone and the cool pressure, my eye immediately felt better.

"You're going to be fine, synok," my mom said, using the Ukrainian word for "son." After about ten minutes, I pulled away the cloth and opened my eye. Everything was blurry. I couldn't see. The tears started to flow for real.

Next thing I knew, I was being examined by an emergency room doctor at the big hospital in Perth Amboy, ten miles up the road. The doctor put a few drops in my eye and looked at it under the bright light. I hadn't spent a lot of time in hospitals, but I could tell from her demeanor that the situation was not looking good. She called for the eye specialist, who did his own examination. More scowls and headshakes. The doctors told the nurse to put a patch over my eye and then they all left the room.

With my good left eye, I took in my surroundings—the bright overhead lights, the infusion pump, the gurneys lined up in the hallway, and the tops of the trees swaying in the breeze outside my window. For the first time in my life, I became aware of my own perception, because it had been suddenly cut in half. Call it addition through subtraction. I began seeing things that were always there, but that I hadn't noticed or had taken for granted.

This went on for close to a week. Every day, the doctors came in and examined my eye. There were never any smiles or warm greetings. No "Hey, TJ, great to see you!" They would check my eye, confer in hushed tones, then walk out of the room without so much as a word to me or my mother. I should mention that my father just so happened to be a few floors up at the same hospital recovering from a back injury he'd sustained in a car accident a week earlier. It had not been a banner week for the Kostecky family. On my fifth day, he was finally able to move around enough to come see me. I remember him walking into the room, gingerly but with a sense of purpose I'd never seen before.

"They want to take your eye out, synok," he said. "They don't think they can save it."

The room started to spin on me. Even though I knew the news wasn't good from the doctors, I never considered the possibility of actually losing my eye. As the information sunk in, the fear for my future made me cry.

"I'm not going to let that happen," my dad said. "I'm getting you out of here."

I still break into tears every time I think back on that moment. There stood my dad, barely able to walk but filled with courage and confidence and displaying complete and utter selflessness. That moment taught me about the importance of sacrifice. My dad would do everything, including risking his own health and safety, for his children. Naturally if he had accepted the doctor's decision, the outcome for me would have been much different. His courage and belief is something I've leaned on throughout my life. When faced with a seemingly insurmountable challenge, I think to myself, "What would my dad do?"

Later that night he checked us out of the hospital and we drove through the Lincoln Tunnel into the bright lights of New York City.

My dad was well connected to the medical community through his work, so I was fortunate to get in with a top doctor at Manhattan Eye and Ear, one of the preeminent hospitals in the world for eye, ear, and throat problems. Despite its reputation, the place was incredibly drab, housed in a turn-of-the-century building in Midtown, with old-fashioned light fixtures and frosted windows that you couldn't see out of, even if you did have perfect vision. It was all in stark contrast to the bright, shiny hospital I'd just come from.

But the staff knew exactly what they were doing. The nurses were all older Irish women and they took a shine to me because I was so much younger than most of the patients there. "Don't you worry your little heart, TJ," they'd say. "Everything is going to be all right."

Shortly after being checked in, a new doctor came to examine my eye.

"You have a very bad infection in your eye," he told me. "Fragments of the nail are lodged in it. That's why you can't see. We're going to have to inject medicine into your eyelid to stop the infection."

My parents both had to work, so I was by myself when the doctor delivered this news. I swallowed hard and nodded my head. Within a few minutes, the old Irish nurse was on one side, holding my left hand, and the doctor was on the other, leaning into my eye with a six-inch needle. I remember sweat pouring down my face. I grabbed the brass lamp on my right and squeezed it for dear life as he gently inserted the needle. If I moved an inch, the needle could miss the mark and that would be it, game over. Talk about pressure. But I held still long enough for the doctor to finish injecting the medicine through the inside of my bottom eyelid. It hurt like hell. Then he repeated the procedure on the top eyelid. That one hurt even more. It was the most painful experience of my life.

Then it was over. And I was alone in the room, for what would be a two-week convalescence. Every few hours a nurse would come in to check my eye and change the dressing. And my parents would visit after work as often as they could. My only other distraction was a small transistor radio, which I used to listen to the Mets. The baseball broadcast trio of Ralph Kiner, Bob Murphy, and Lindsey Nelson got me through a lot of dark, lonely nights.

During the day, I observed what I could with my left eye, as I had at the first hospital, only at a much more heightened level. It was like in the comic books where the hero first discovers their superpower and has to figure out how to use it. All of a sudden, my head was on a swivel, turning to see objects and people outside my line of vision. It forced me to look longer, more closely, more deeply. You often hear about when people lose one sense, other senses are heightened. If they go completely blind, for example, their hearing becomes more acute. A similar process happened, but all within my vision. Because I had a narrower field of vision to work with, I had to work harder to gather detailed information: a person's facial expressions, how they moved their lips, their body language, their show of emotion, and so on. All this information that I never noticed before was suddenly right in front of me. Within seconds of the doctors or nurses entering the room, I could tell if there was worry or relief in their minds.

As the days progressed, I received daily injections and my recovery continued. There was more joy in their faces. The treatment was working. My eye was getting better.

"You still have a long road ahead and your vision is never going to be perfect," the doctor said to me toward the end of my two-week stint at the hospital. He was right. For the next three months I had to wear a patch over my eye, and for six months after that I needed sunglasses anytime I left the house. Even then, my eyesight was 20/100 at best, meaning lots of things were still blurry. And that's how it is today, actually even worse, given the passage of time.

What I came to appreciate in that hospital room, and in the months and years that followed, is the difference between sight and vision. We are all able to open our eyes and see the world around us. But seeing is only part of it. We then have to process all the information that our eyes send to our brain. This is the power of perception. And most people only tap into a small fraction of it.

That's how you can have twenty-two players on a soccer field and one of them sees things that no one else can see. It's also why some managers get so much more out of their team than others. Or why some doctors are able to spot the diagnosis that others missed. In each case, these people are using the power of perception to elevate their vision.

It's easy to think of this power as a God-given gift, something you're either born with or not. My life's work is showing how nothing could be further from the truth. It started on the soccer field, where I've used Vision Training to help thousands of players see the field better. And it continues with my work as a mentor and life coach, where my Vision Training for Life program helps people in all walks of life become the transformational leaders they want to be.

It took a nail to the eye for me to unlock my own power of perception. You don't need to go through anything so gruesome. That's why I wrote this book.

Chapter Two

A SHARED VISION

ast-forward to 1980. I'm at Front Row, a sports bar in East Rutherford, New Jersey, not far from the Meadowlands Sports Complex, known today as MetLife Stadium. It was the heyday of the New York Cosmos, which the journalist Gavin Newsham called "the most glamorous team in world football." These guys were legit, with players like Pelé, Franz Beckenbauer, Carlos Alberto Torres, Johan Neeskens, and Wim Rijsbergen. Talk about dream teams.

In the years following my eye accident, soccer had become my passion. I was always an all-sports kid—I loved going to New York Rangers hockey and Knicks basketball games with my dad and listening to the Mets broadcasts on the radio. But soccer was the game I played. I discovered it through the Ukrainian Sitch Sports Summer Camp I attended in the Catskills, where it was played religiously, along with volleyball, another sport with strong European ties. I could hit an effective crosscourt spike in volleyball, but my teen years were all about soccer.

I had a decent first touch, which along with my keen sense of vision and overall feel for the game, not to mention hours upon hours of hard work, were enough for All-County honors my senior year in high school. But I sensed early on that my soccer journey would lead to coaching. So I became a true student of the game. I watched the European clubs on television whenever I could, which back then wasn't a lot. I read any books and articles I could get my hands on, including *Soccer America*, the soccer bible whose arrival to the mailbox I eagerly awaited each week. And, of course, my dad and I went to every New York Cosmos game.

On one remarkable occasion I even managed to get into the locker room. It wasn't like it is today, where you need a dozen credentials to get anywhere near the players. I was nineteen years old, and my best friend, Donnie Maggi (a different Donnie from the nail incident), scored passes to a Cosmos practice and press conference. There I was in the locker room after training with a scrum of reporters and sweaty players; a few of the internationals were puffing on cigarettes (the players, not the reporters), which blew me away. It was the start of preseason training and the team had underperformed the year before, losing in the Soccer Bowl final. Most of the questions were provocative: Why wasn't Bogie defending more? Why wasn't Brcic getting more minutes in goal?

I really wanted to ask a question but was nervous as hell. At that time, I was a quiet teenager and afraid to embarrass myself. Nevertheless, this was a chance to speak to some of the best in the world so I raised my hand from the back of the room. Wim Rijsbergen, the great Dutch defender, pointed to me from his locker. He had come to the Cosmos in '79 after a successful career with Feyenoord in

Holland's top division, as well as starring with the Dutch National Team.

"What's your question, kid?" he asked.

I was petrified. Talk about legends. Wim was one of the finest defenders in the world and played behind the great Johan Cruyff during the '74 and '78 World Cups. Holland made the final both times, only to lose to Germany and Argentina, respectively.

"Thank you, Wim," I said. I had made up my mind earlier that if I got this opportunity, I was going to ask a soccer question. The reporters in the room didn't know the game. They'd been given the assignment by their editors to go cover the Cosmos and so here they were, dutifully going through the motions, hoping for a juicy quote or two to bring back to the office.

"My question is this," I continued. "Are the Cosmos playing Total Futbol?" I was referring to the Dutch style of play that revolutionized the game, a free-flowing, player-centric tactical system where any outfield player can take over the role of any other player in a team. It was about using 360-degree vision to see the entire field of play, not just your one corner of the action. Like the questions from the reporters, the Cosmos' answers at the presser had been pretty rote up until that point. But in response to my question, Wim's eyes lit up. He became very animated and growled, "Absolutely not!"

The coach of the Cosmos at the time was the famous German gaffer Hennes Weisweiler. He preferred a more traditional, structured style of play over new age Total Futbol. At that point, I glanced over at the gaffer, and everyone in the locker room saw his body language stiffen.

I asked Wim to say more and we got into a lively discussion of the various merits of Total Futbol, as the reporters furiously scribbled away in their notepads. Weisweiler wandered off. The presser wound down shortly after that. As everyone filed out of the room, Wim came over to me and said, "I have to take a shower. You stay here. I want to talk some more with you."

Sure enough, Wim came back after his shower and we talked soccer for another twenty minutes. And then he gave me his phone number. The Cosmos were heading to the Bahamas for more preseason training, but they'd be back in three weeks.

"Give me a call; we'll talk again," he said.

You better believe I did. True to his word, Wim invited me over to his apartment in Jersey City, overlooking the Manhattan skyline. I walked in the door and there on the couch in just his practice shorts, watching the New York Mets, was Johan Neeskens, another Dutch great who scored the lone goal in their 2–1 loss to Germany in the '74 World Cup final. It was freakin' surreal! A nineteen-year-old college kid from Jersey hanging out with two of the best players in the world.

"Hey, how are you doing?" Johan asked.

I played it cool, but in my head I was thinking, "Holy crap, this is amazing!" That's how soccer in America was back then. As Johan told me later that day, when he played for Barcelona he couldn't step outside without getting mauled by fans wanting an autograph. But on the streets of New York City, nobody knew who he was. This was one of the main reasons he chose to play there— to get a break from the spotlight. I spent several hours with these two incredibly kind and approachable stars. I was impressed by how "human" they were and also how much curiosity they had for American sports, and all aspects of American culture. Johan had told me that he loved watching baseball and as a kid he played on the Dutch youth national baseball team. At one point he had to make a choice between the two sports he loved, and only chose soccer because baseball was a minor sport in Holland, the way soccer was in the U.S.

I knew that was going to eventually change; soccer is too great a sport and the U.S. too big a country. There was an opportunity for me to get in on the ground floor and influence the growth of the game. So I continued with my informal education, while also earning a U.S. Soccer national "C" coaching license. At the age of twenty, I started the Jefferson Youth Soccer Club in Oak Ridge, New Jersey. The sport was still so young that many towns around the country had yet to introduce the game.

All these things were going on in my life as I jockeyed for a position at the bar at the Front Row. The Cosmos had just won a thrilling playoff match against the Los Angeles Aztecs, 3–1, so the mood was loud, festive, and rowdy for the post-match celebration. Fans always poured into the Front Row because the players would go there too.

I was just about to order a Heineken when I heard the guy in front of me say, "Stolichnaya." He was a wiry dude with smooth tan skin, just like a baby's, and a big head of curly hair. Americans always destroy the pronunciation of this Soviet-era vodka. But this was flawless. In fact, to my ear it could have been my dad or my grandfather. As he walked past me with his drink, I said to him, "You ordered that like a Ukrainian."

"That's because I am Ukrainian." He smiled. "What, is it written on my face?"

"I'm Ukrainian too," I said with a huge grin.

"Oh yeah? Where are you from?" he asked.

"Let me order a beer and I'll tell you," I said.

That's how I met Len Bilous, the Venezuelan-raised soccer player, an Einstein of coaching and my eventual cofounder of Vision

Training Soccer. As I learned that night at Front Row, Len was following up a successful playing stint in the American Soccer League with an even better career in coaching. In fact, he'd recently been named Coach of the Year in the professional Major Indoor Soccer League.

I was impressed by his accomplishments, but what drew me most to Len was the way he looked at the game. Immediately, I could feel that we were kindred spirits. We saw eye to eye from the very start, though he was ten years older with much more wisdom and game experience. He would become my mentor, my Yoda.

"How about Beckenbauer tonight?" he said to me during our first chat.

"Something else," I responded.

"Even when he was twenty-five, Franzie wasn't the fastest or the strongest," Len continued. "Here he is at thirty-five years old and even slower. His physical skills are diminishing and yet he's still playing at an extraordinary level against guys who are ten and fifteen years younger."

"It's freakish," I agreed.

"It is," Len said. "But I've been analyzing Franz for years now, along with other top players. The one thing they all have in common is lightning-fast decision-making. They are taking in information more quickly than their opponents and it's allowing them to always stay one step ahead."

"You're absolutely right, Len, that's exactly it," I said. "And when you consistently make smart decisions on the soccer field, it allows for so much more creativity and improvisation. Those qualities above all else are missing from American soccer."

"Spoken like a true Ukrainian," he said with a wink.

Len and I exchanged phone numbers and agreed to stay in

touch. In the weeks that followed, I continued to reflect on our conversation. I wanted to understand why so many soccer players in this country lacked sound decision-making ability. The answer I kept coming back to was coaching.

American sports are filled with overcoaching. Think about the big three—football, baseball, basketball. They are all coach-centric. In football, you have half a dozen coaches in the booth relaying information to the head coach and his assistants on the sidelines, who then pass on instructions to the forty-million-dollar-a-year quarterback on the field. In baseball, when the batter comes to the plate, what does he do? He looks to the third base coach who is telling him what to do by tapping his shoulder or touching his belt. And in basketball there's the coach, often in a fine pressed suit, pacing up and down the sideline, barking orders to his obedient players.

When soccer started to become popular in the U.S. in the '70s and '80s, it took on this same coach-driven mentality. And why wouldn't it? Especially at the youth level, most of the coaches were parents who had grown up playing American sports where coaches did all the talking—or shouting, more often. So that's what they did.

But soccer is a different game. It is twenty-two players engaged in ninety minutes of uninterrupted play. There are no time-outs, no team huddles. The sport is often compared to ballet, in part because it's so beautiful to watch (the beautiful game, they call it), with its combination of balance, improvisation, and footwork, but also because it's a continuous movement of interconnected players. More than any other sport, soccer is a case where the whole is greater than the sum of its parts.

In their fascinating book *The Numbers Game*, economists Chris Anderson and David Sally support this idea through an analysis of the strong link / weak link principle. To do so, they compare soccer with basketball. The latter is a strong-link sport, meaning a team's success is largely determined by its best player. Think of LeBron James carrying the Cleveland Cavaliers on his back to an NBA Championship in 2016 and Nikola Jokić doing the same with the Denver Nuggets in 2023. Or Michael Jordan's six rings a generation earlier. Can anyone name the fifth starter from any of those teams? I know I can't. Basketball is a sport where, more often than not, the team with the biggest superstar wins.

Soccer, by comparison, is a weak-link sport, meaning most teams are only as good as their eleventh player. Sure, there are moments where Mbappé, Messi, or Maradona dribbles the length of the field and scores an absolute wonder goal. But more often than not, goals are scored following a buildup of play where several players touch the ball. It's not unusual for a team to string together six to seven passes before the ball finds the back of the net. That can't happen if one or two weaker players keep giving the ball away.

This interdependence and flow of play makes soccer a weak-link sport. It also makes it player driven. Don't get me wrong—proper coaching and team management are essential. But once the whistle blows, it's up to the players to make good, fast, and accurate decisions *on their own*, without a coach or teammate telling them what to do.

Go to any soccer field in America, especially at the youth level, and you'll hear a cacophony of commands: "Pass!" "Shoot!" "Here!" "Turn!" "Man on!" As I like to say, do you think Kylian Mbappé needs anyone to tell him "man on"? No! He already knows because he's constantly scanning the field, taking in information at the speed of light, 186,000 miles per second. Voice commands coming in by sound, or at 767 miles per hour, are way too slow and no use to him.

These were the light bulbs that went off in my mind after that first meeting with Len. I couldn't wait to continue the conversation, so a few weeks later I visited the farm in rural Connecticut that he was renting for the summer.

I pulled in after dark and Len had a bonfire going in the back field. We pulled up a couple stools, cracked open our beers, and picked up the conversation that we left off in the bar. I shared a memory that our talk had sparked about seeing Pelé play with the Cosmos at Yankee Stadium when I was fifteen years old. He scored a bicycle kick that day, which was amazing to see. But what stuck with me was a far more subtle moment in the second half.

"Pelé is playing center forward and his teammate, the right back, delivers a hard-driven ball from just outside his own box," I explained. "The opposing center back is marking Pelé like white on rice as he makes a diagonal run and drifts toward the ball. Like all thirty thousand fans in the stadium that day, he was waiting for Pelé to collect the ball and turn to goal or lay it off for a supporting mid-fielder. But instead of taking the ball down, he sprints right past it, pulling the defender with him."

"He dummied the ball," Len said

"Yeah, he dummied a thirty-five-yard laser," I continued. "For a second everyone froze, including Pelé's left winger. But then he and everyone in Yankee Stadium realized what Pelé had just done and what was happening as a result, as the ball took a couple bounces and started rolling toward the left corner flag. The winger took off down the field with the right back in fast pursuit."

"Without even touching the ball, Pelé had intentionally helped his team move the ball eighty yards up the field," Len said. "I was there that day as well. Everyone in the stadium was fooled. But not you."

"Not you either, I guess," I said.

We talked long into the night, as the bonfire turned to a pile of embers. I shared my eye accident, and how it had broadened my lens and shifted my perspective.

"We tend to think of vision as this natural ability that you either have or don't have," Len said. "That's a bunch of BS. It can absolutely be learned." He then talked about his own experience as a player. It was late in his career, well past his prime, that he started studying Beckenbauer, Pelé, Cruyff, and other field virtuosos with exceptional vision.

"I said to myself, let me see if I can train myself to not look at the ball as much," he explained. "Because from the first moment we step on the field, everyone says to focus on the ball. So I started knocking the ball against a brick wall. As soon as the ball started coming back to me, I would take a quick peek over my shoulder. At first, it was very uncomfortable. But after a few days it became easier and more natural. I was playing in a Sunday league. I swear to you, TJ, the next time out I was 50 percent better. My decisions were 50 percent faster. My teammates were like, 'Len, what did you have for breakfast this morning? You were on fire out there.'"

That was the "aha" moment for me. My eye injury had made me so much more attuned to the world around me, as my love and devotion for the game of soccer was growing. Sitting by the fire with my newfound Yoda figure, I suddenly understood the critical role vision has in the context of the game. "Don't look where everyone else is looking," Len was saying. "Look where everyone isn't. That's the secret, young man." In my head I'm like, "Holy smokes, you're right! You're absolutely right!"

Six months later, Len and I started our first summer camps in Jefferson Township and Roxbury, New Jersey. We called it Soccer Magic, because that's what we delivered. By getting our kids to look and scan, they magically became better soccer players. That first summer we had maybe thirty-five kids ages nine to thirteen across the two camps. Every activity was designed to get them to play "eyes up" ball. There was no shouting, clapping, or calling for the ball. In a variation on Len's wall ball drill, we'd play a ball into a player's feet with a coach standing behind them, holding up one or two fingers. The player had to check their shoulder and gather data the moment the ball was delivered. A more advanced version substituted the coach for a defender, who would either close in on the receiving player as the ball was played or stand a few feet back. By checking the position of the defender, the receiving player knew whether to play an early one-touch pass to maintain possession or collect the ball, turn, and engage the defender.

These exercises empowered players to make the right decision, which in turn allowed for more creativity and improvisation. Without a bunch of people screaming "MAN ON!", they played calm, relaxed, and creative soccer. By the end of the week, every single camper had improved by leaps and bounds. It wasn't magic at all. It was a simple shift in perspective. With that, Vision Training was born.

Proof Positive of the Power of Vision Training

I'm often asked which American soccer player has the best vision of all time. Tab Ramos and Landon Donovan are in the conversation. Hugo Pérez back in the day. On the women's side, you have Carli Loyd, Mia Hamm, and Julie Foudy. These are all outstanding soccer players. But for my money, there's one player in a field by himself when it comes to seeing the game: Claudio Reyna.

It's possible I'm biased, since I had the privilege of coaching Claudio as a youth player in New Jersey. But I bet if you put this question to ten authorities of the game, most would cast their vote for Claudio. He was so good at seeing the field that he led the U.S. Men's National Team to the quarterfinals of the 2002 World Cup and was voted one of the top eleven players in the world by his peers.

I first met Claudio in 1986, when he was a thirteen-year-old trying out for New Jersey's Olympic Development Program (ODP). Back then, this was the single pathway to the U.S. national teams. Each state had a team, and the best players from each would go on to compete at the regional level—Northeast, South, Midwest, and West. And then, the very best would be selected to represent the U.S. in international competitions.

I was twenty-six at the time, a good five years into Vision Training (our camps were now growing and fielding three hundred to four hundred kids), and I'd been coaching at the high school level for a few years. The guy who coached the U-14 ODP program was head coach of Randolph High School, and he asked me to come on as an assistant. In '87, I took over as head coach. That put me in good company with several legends of U.S. coaching, guys like Bob Bradley, who ran the men's program at Princeton University and would later go on to coach the U.S. Men's National Team at the 2010 World Cup. And Manny Schellscheidt, the "godfather of U.S. coaches," and one of the first coaches in the U.S. to earn his A license, the highest in the land. The two of them oversaw Northeast Region One.

Claudio was one of over 150 kids to try out for New Jersey's Under-14 ODP team. His father was Argentinian, so he used to take Claudio back home to Buenos Aires to train with Club Atlético Independiente every summer. You could see the pedigree right away (and it's obviously continued down the line to Claudio's son Gio, an equally talented attacking player for the U.S. National Team). Claudio's ball skills were exceptional and he had very good vision for his age, especially within fifteen to twenty yards. A lot of the work I did with him early on was getting him to expand his vision.

"You have no trouble finding spaces and picking out passes at close range," I told him before a match, shortly after I transitioned to head coach. "Today I want you to go out there and see how many times you can find a teammate that's thirty yards away with one or two touches." Lo and behold, he went out there and did just that. And not just once or twice. Throughout the match he expanded his vision and connected half a dozen balls into deep space.

There are no shortage of moments from Claudio's highlight reel at ODP. But one play really stands out. He was fourteen, and we'd been working together now for a second year. His vision had gone from exceptional to off the charts. We were playing an exhibition match in Hightstown, New Jersey, against an all-star team of New York's best players who were on their way to play against top European clubs overseas. Their holding midfielder was an absolute beast who was tasked with marking Claudio. Halfway through the second half, one of our outside backs pinged a ball to Claudio, who was right on the touchline at midfield. Claudio checked his shoulder and saw the defender closing in fast. As he looked back to the ball, it took a funny hop and skipped toward the defender.

Any other player would have kicked the ball away to avoid the turnover. Instead, Claudio calmly and gently flicked the ball up over the defender's foot just as he was about to reach it. The defender charged past him like a bull. As cool as a matador, Claudio stepped around him, collected the loose ball, and switched the field with a thirty-yard driven pass into space. It was such a subtle moment, but it showed Claudio's genius and his ability to make quick and accurate decisions under pressure by constantly expanding his vision and taking in information.

As singular a talent as Claudio was, he almost didn't make it to the regional stage. At the culmination of each ODP season, teams from each state compete in one final tournament. In 1988, this event took place in Binghamton, New York. Our New Jersey squad, with Claudio at center midfield, hadn't lost a game all year. We'd been implementing Vision Training for two years now and the players applied it so well that other teams struggled to take the ball away. It was like the old Barcelona teams with Xavi, Iniesta, and Messi.

The regional coaches included Bradley, Schellscheidt, and Ron McEachen, another legendary U.S. coach who at the time ran the men's program at the University of Vermont and would go on to serve as the assistant coach of the New England Revolution in Major League Soccer.

The first half ended in a nil–nil draw. As I was walking to speak to the boys, Ron pulled me aside. Out of a pool of a couple hundred players across fourteen states, he had to pick the top eighteen to send on to the regionals in Colorado the following weekend. It was a challenging and difficult process. Those who don't make it get lost in the shuffle and likely never have this chance again.

"We're not sure about Reyna," Ron said to me, not mincing words. "We just don't know if he's good enough to bring to the regional team. He doesn't seem to impact the game. What do you think of him, TJ?"

For all his talent and ability, Claudio wasn't the flashiest player on the pitch. Because of his quiet personality, he often flew under the radar. From my perspective, that was another part of his strength, his stealth ability to strike at any time. But I could see why the coaches might not be convinced.

"Ron, I promise you, he's good enough," I said.

"Okay, TJ, I appreciate it," Ron said. "But we're still not convinced."

After the halftime huddle, I held Claudio back. "How bad do you want to make the regional team?" I asked him.

"I want to make it, Coach," he said, looking up at me with his big puppy dog eyes.

I turned to the stands, pointed, and said, "Well, you have forty-five minutes to show these coaches that you belong."

What happened next? He went out there and absolutely crushed it. He dominated the midfield, slipping sublime through balls, winning 50-50 chances, and disrupting their counterattack. We won the match, 1–0. Claudio got the regional call-up. The following week, I flew to Colorado Springs to support the six guys from Jersey playing for Region One, the most of any state—another testament to the power of Vision Training. Claudio continued to tear it up, scoring a goal and an assist in a 2–2 draw against the current U-16 National Team.

The next day, he was training with the U-16 National Team. Six months later, Claudio was in Scotland to compete in the 1989 FIFA U-16 World Cup, where Team USA beat Brazil for the first time ever in international play. It was the launching pad for Claudio's career. And to think it might not have happened. If he didn't make regionals, that could have been it.

I caught up with Claudio a few weeks after the Scotland tournament.

"What was it like over there?" I asked him.

"My vision made all the difference," he said, words I'll never forget. "The players were so much faster; there was such little time and space on the ball," he continued. "Without the awareness, I would have been lost out there. Vision was the thing. And, TJ, you and my dad are the only ones who have ever taught it to me."

I share this story about Claudio because it was a huge moment of validation for me and Len and our efforts around Vision Training. As a twenty-five-year-old youth soccer coach, I believed in the program, even though most coaches did not, and some even ridiculed it to my face. But so much of it took place in a kind of soccer laboratory of camps and developmental training sessions. Claudio was proof positive that it worked.

But there's more to the Claudio story than soccer. A lot of things had to happen to get him to Colorado Springs, and onto the field in Scotland, and then on to one of the most decorated careers in U.S. soccer history. For starters, Claudio had to be willing to learn, not just from me, but from his father and Manny Schellscheidt and any number of coaches and players who came into his orbit. Ron McEachen had to have enough trust in me, at the time a twenty-five-year-old nobody with not a lot of coaching credibility, to ask for my take on Claudio. It would have been very easy for Ron to think to himself, "I don't care what this high school coach has to say." But he recognized that I was curious, open to learn, and engaged, and so he valued my opinion. Then, in that brief moment at halftime, I had to find a way to inspire Claudio and he had to be open to the message.

None of these things on their own might seem like much. But when you put them all together, the result is magic. What the Claudio experience helped me understand was that the magic of Vision Training isn't limited to soccer. The same process must be applied to the game of life.

Chapter Three

BEYOND THE
SOCCER PITCH

As I entered the bright lecture hall in the Entrepreneurship Center of LIU's Brooklyn campus, more than a hundred students and faculty were already milling about. The Center was a kind of think tank where corporate leaders from the outside world gave talks, pitched ideas, and generally elevated the conversation on campus. The speaker that day was from BuzzFeed, the media company, and the topic was cultivating purpose throughout your career.

A few decades had passed since my earliest coaching days with the likes of Claudio Reyna, so I was pretty far along in my career. In fact, I'd been at LIU for close to twenty years at that point, turning the Division I men's soccer program into a perennial powerhouse in the competitive Northeast Conference. The year prior, our 2015 squad had posted its first-ever in-conference undefeated season, which earned the team a berth in the NCAA tournament, and our group NEC Coaching Staff of the Year honors.

Besides coaching, in the offseason, I was teaching several undergraduate courses in the Sport Management Program that I cofounded: Sport Psychology 101, Principles and Philosophy of Coaching, and a graduate-level course, Principles of Sports Branding. As an educator and life learner, I was curious and excited to hear what an executive from BuzzFeed had to share about his own journey. I grabbed a seat at the back of the hall.

In a moment of synchronicity (something I'll talk about at length later in the book), I was struck by how much the BuzzFeed guy looked like a young Len Bilous, with his big head of curly hair, olive complexion, and warm, friendly smile.

"Before I get started," the speaker said, "I want to invite you all to chime in at any point during the presentation with ideas or comments. I'm here to learn too." I'd never heard someone do that before. It was an endearing and effective show of vulnerability. The talk that followed was equally engaging, weaving actionable advice into a compelling story of a career that had taken him all over the world.

As the man was wrapping up, he once again solicited feedback from the crowd. I raised my hand from the back row.

"Yes, sir," the man said.

"First of all, I want to say how much I loved your presentation," I began. "I learned a great deal and I'm sure the students around me did as well."

"Thank you," he said.

"Can I make one small suggestion?" I asked. Everyone in the lecture hall turned to look at me.

"Of course," he replied.

"In your ninth slide, you gave the advice to always network with the CEO's administrative assistant, because that person is the gatekeeper, with a finger on the pulse of the organization, not to mention the boss's schedule. This is great advice. But can I suggest that you replace the word 'network' with 'connect'? Because when you network with someone, it's more of a transactional relationship. *What can you do for me?* Whereas when you connect with someone, it's transformational, with meaning and purpose on both sides of the relationship. *What can I do for you?*"

There was a brief silence when I finished talking. And then everyone in the hall started to clap. I was a little taken aback. The transformational-versus-transactional divide is something I'd been thinking and talking about for years. It's core to my personal belief system, so much so that I figured other people felt the same way. Here were a hundred people who perhaps were hearing it for the first time.

"I'm going to change it right now," the man said. Sure enough, he walked over to his laptop, opened his deck to the ninth slide, and replaced the word "network" with "connect."

As this was happening, I noticed an older gentleman out of the corner of my eye in a three-piece suit. He had turned in my direction along with everyone else in the hall and now he was still looking my way. I smiled hesitantly, thinking he was perhaps trying to get the attention of someone behind me.

"Will you come speak to my class?" he said. The question was clearly directed at me.

"Who, me?" I replied. "About what?"

"About anything you want," he said.

That's how I met Norman Schwartz, who would become one

of the most important mentors in a lifetime filled with them. We were both late for classes during that first encounter, so we agreed to meet for lunch later that week, at Junior's Restaurant in downtown Brooklyn, right across the street from campus. Over towering pastrami sandwiches, I learned the details of Norman's remarkable life in business, which had started fifty years earlier after his graduation from LIU. He talked about the various companies he'd started and led and how he retired in his thirties to travel the world before coming back to New York City and joining the faculty at LIU.

"That's fascinating, Norman," I said, as the waiter cleared away our plates. "So tell me. Your management class on global studies ... what do you want me to talk about?"

"You've obviously had an interesting career as a coach and mentor," Norman said. "Those skills and qualities are more important than ever. Why don't you talk about how to become the best possible leader you can be? Honestly, it sounds to me like you've been doing that your whole life."

"Whoa," I thought to myself. Norman was right. My coaching philosophy, based on the principles of Vision Training, has always been about helping my players approach the game with their eyes wide open so that they can make smart decisions and form strong connections on the field. As the experience with Reyna from thirty years earlier demonstrated, these same principles can be applied to life off the field to find meaning and form the human interactions we all crave. I realized that I had been doing it my whole life.

After lunch with Norman, I couldn't wait to get back home and start pulling together my ideas into a coherent presentation. A week later I was standing in Norman's classroom in LIU's School of Business. The university attracts students from all backgrounds and stages of life, so as I looked out over the room there was a mix of traditional and nontraditional students staring back at me.

"Here we go," I thought, and jumped into the presentation, starting with a slide on integrity, and a favorite quote from Alan Simpson, the former U.S. senator from Wyoming: "If you have integrity, nothing else matters. If you don't have integrity, nothing else matters." I thought it teed up the rest of my talk nicely. Based on all the nodding in the room, it seemed to have landed.

I won't go into any more detail about the talk that day because, after all, that's what this book is for. But I want to share one other moment from that day. It occurred about midway through the presentation as I was talking about motivation and the power of behavior modeling.

"In your own life journey, I want you all to think about someone who saw something in you that you didn't see in yourself," I told the class. I then made my way around the room, calling on different students to share their experience. One talked about a special teacher in middle school, another about her favorite aunt, a third about his teammate from the baseball team, who happened to be sitting right next to him. Then I reached a middle-aged woman who was part of a continuing education program at the university. As I got closer to her chair, I noticed she was crying.

"Are you okay?" I asked, putting a hand on her shoulder.

"Yes, I'm sorry," she said. "It's just that I realize I've never had anyone believe in me."

For a moment I felt terrible. I'd come to the classroom that day to elevate these students' lives and instead here I was bringing one of them to tears. Then I caught myself, shifted my perspective, and recognized the teaching opportunity that was taking place.

"I'm deeply sorry to hear that," I told the woman. "But on the other hand, you just realized a powerful lesson."

"What's that?" she said, looking up at me.

"The most important lesson is to always believe in yourself," I said.

She nodded, put her pen down on the table, and gently closed her eyes. I could tell that she heard me and that the brief connection between us was going to move her life in a new direction. I'm not saying all her troubles were going to suddenly disappear. But the slight shift in perspective would help her see and find new possibilities.

As the workshop finished, the energy in the room was magnetic. The students were full of smiles and appreciation as they filed out. Norman approached me from the back of the room.

"You were awesome," he said.

"Thank you, Norman," I replied. "I appreciate you."

"No, no, no, you don't understand," he pressed. "I've been doing this for decades. I've heard people who get ten grand to talk for an hour. You're as good or better than any of them."

I could tell Norman really meant what he said. Through a lifetime of coaching and mentoring, I knew the power of validation. So while Norman's praise made me blush, I also recognized the gravity of this moment. Just as I had helped the middle-aged woman in my workshop see herself in a different light, Norman was showing me a new path forward for myself. I knew I had to take it.

That's when Vision Training for Life was officially born—even if it had been gestating for decades. Word spread quickly on campus about the workshop I'd given. One of Norman's students swam for LIU, so the next week I spoke to the swim team. LIU's head baseball coach caught wind, so next up was the baseball team. In the years since, I've given dozens of workshops to a wide range of groups and organizations, from the New York City's Athletic Directors Association to the Commissioner's Office of the NCAA DI Northeast Conference to the staff at Ken Wright Cellars, a world-renowned winery in Carlton, Oregon, and to the deans at Bard College in Annandale-on-Hudson, New York.

The lessons I impart and the stories I tell are relevant to anyone in a leadership position—bosses, managers, coaches, teachers, parents, students, and athletes, really most of us when you get right down to it, because we're all connected in one way or another, like the twenty-two players on a soccer pitch moving through space and time together. But the biggest takeaway I want for anyone reading this book is becoming the leader of their own life. It's about self-empowerment and the belief that you can have the life you want.

In the pages that follow, I'll lay out the basic program for taking your life to the next level by expanding your field of vision and being open and ready for every opportunity. As I tell my players, the work you do off the ball is what sets you up for success in the big game moments. This book is that work. Reading it will improve your life. That's my promise to you.

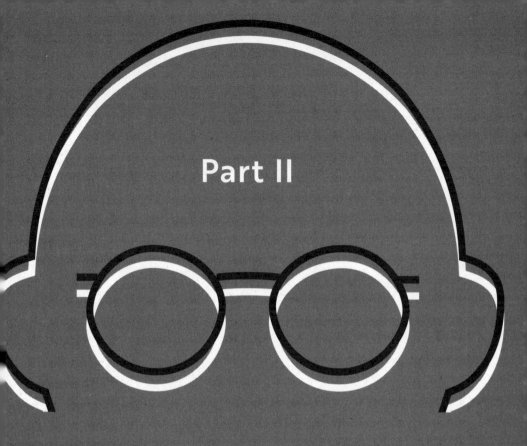

Part II

THE SEVEN
LESSONS
OF GREAT
LEADERSHIP

Chapter Four

SEE THE WHOLE FIELD

The Five Ps of Vision Training

By the early 2000s, some twenty years after Len and I opened our first Vision Training program in New Jersey, word of the training had spread throughout the U.S. and even around the world. One morning in 2006, I opened my inbox and saw an email from a coach named Kari Raita, who ran a youth soccer program in Turku, a beautiful old city on the southwest coast of Finland.

Kari had come across Vision Training online, bought the training video Len and I had produced, and was writing to see if we would ever run a course in Turku. Synchronicity, the universe had responded. It just so happened that I was planning a recruiting trip to Finland in three months, so I agreed to put on a course for him at the same time.

A few months later, following a successful recruiting voyage around Scandinavia, I arrived in Turku, where I was met by the woman who served as a lead liaison with the club. I had sent a bunch of our videos beforehand so that I wasn't lugging them all over Finland. She was holding one of the DVDs in her hand.

"What does 'vision' mean?" she asked. "We don't have that exact word in Finnish."

"No word for vision?" I said in amazement, then did my best to translate the work we did in our courses and camps, helping players see the entire field of play in order to make smart, well-informed decisions based on the information they were taking in.

"Oh, I see," she said. "We call that 'perception' here."

"Perception," I said. "Exactly."

I'll come back to the Finland story. For now, I want to stay on the word "perception," since it's the core building block to my program. As I continued to codify Vision Training over the years, I realized that there is more to the process beyond perception. Yes, playing "eyes up" soccer is key to gathering data, but what you do with that information is equally important. As is your ability to execute based on the information you receive. And to do all this on a consistent basis.

After thinking on all this for literally decades, and getting input from countless coaches and players across all sports, and also from casual observers of the "beautiful game," I ultimately landed on an action plan that encompasses the entire cycle of Vision Training. This is what I call the Five Ps: Perceive, Process, Plan, Perform, Persist. As I made the transition from Vision Training Soccer into Vision Training for Life, I saw how the Five Ps worked equally for both. I'm now going to take you through the cycle, showing you what the Five Ps look like on the soccer pitch and in the field of life.

I call it a cycle, but the better image might be pistons firing in syn-chronized movement, each playing a vital part in driving the engine of our lives forward.

The First P: Perceive

"Can you go out there and get five looks every ten seconds?"

That's the challenge I give my players every time they take the field. My goal is to get them to play with their head on a swivel so that they're in a constant state of information gathering. Picture a five-year-old kid from Anywhere, America, dribbling a soccer ball for the first time. They're getting zero looks every ten seconds be-cause their eyes are pinned to the ball. At a certain point in their de-velopment, they'll hopefully learn to pick their head up so that they can see where they're running, giving them one, maybe two looks every ten seconds. For a lot of players, that's as good as it gets. Sure, there are a few exceptions who figure out how to get to three to four looks on their own. But for the most part, youth players in the U.S. are not trained or conditioned, nor is it demanded of them, to scan the field, and so they play the game with the blinders fixed in place. (Quick side note to coaches and players: If there's room in your bud-get for training flags, use them as much as possible during dribbling drills. It will force your players to dribble with their **eyes up!**)

The best ballers in the world, by contrast, constantly have their head on a swivel. Arsène Wenger, the legendary Arsenal manager, once spoke about this at a conference in Paris, referring to it as the "radar" effect that the best players possess. "I try to see what happens to a player in the ten seconds before he gets the ball, how many times he takes information and the quality of information he takes," he explained to the crowd. "Very good players scan six to eight times in the ten seconds before getting the ball and normal ones three to four times."

The research into scanning gets even more granular. As part of a study by Professor Geir Jordet from the Norwegian School of Sport Sciences, he analyzed 250 professional footballers for their visual movements in the single second before receiving the ball. Liverpool legend Steven Gerrard managed 0.61 searches per second. Chelsea's Frank Lampard was even better with 0.62 searches per second. Barcelona's Xavi was best with 0.83 searches per second.

I don't want my guys' heads to explode, so I don't worry them with looks per second. But I do demand that they strive to get at least those five looks every ten seconds. When they first join my team, most of them are hearing this all for the first time. They've never been told to scan the field of play. As a result, they're getting two or three looks at most. Like my partner Len all those years ago, playing in a Sunday league match after checking his shoulder while hitting the ball against the wall, their performance improves by 10 to 20 percent from day one. My promise to you: the effect is instant and dramatic. To all readers involved in the game—players, coaches, parents alike—if you take away just one lesson from this book, let it be the need to get in at least five looks every ten seconds.

Of course, I hope you'll get a lot more out of this book, including the ability to be more perceptive as you pass through your daily lives. Everything we do in life is based on vision. How much do you take in? How far ahead can you see? How much can you imagine about who you want to become? To answer these questions, you need to harness your vision.

On the field, it starts with five looks. In life, it's also about being as perceptive as possible as you move throughout your day, especially in your interactions with others. You may have heard the adage that 90 percent of communication is nonverbal. It's a little more complicated than that. Albert Mehrabian, a pioneer researcher of body language in the 1960s, found that communication is 55 percent nonverbal. Whatever the actual percentage, the point is that a huge amount of information is contained in things like eye contact, facial expressions, and hand and body movements. Unless you're attuned to it, you'll miss it.

On the soccer field, we talk about scanning. In real life, we call it "reading the room," something I do all the time. I might notice that one of my players' energy seems a bit off. I'll either go talk to him myself or have an assistant or a captain engage with him. In the classroom, if a student seems distracted, I'll make a point of calling on them early in the lesson to bring them back into the moment. And I'm constantly mindful of my own nonverbal communications. You may have had the experience where someone thought you were angry or upset because of something in your expression or body language, when in fact you were merely deep in thought. By using perception to become self-aware of these nonverbal cues, you can deliver the right message into your universe. Just as greater perception can make you a better reader of other people and situations you encounter throughout your daily life.

Testimonials on the Power of Perception

Since the very beginning of Vision Training, I've always solicited feedback from players and coaches who have gone through the program, either in camp or as a member of one of my teams. Over the years, so much of the feedback has been along these lines: "The game slows down, I'm relaxed," and "I'm so much more confident on the ball," and "It's so much easier to maintain possession since we're not all shouting for the ball and giving away our position on the field."

I love the testimonial I received from a fortysomething guy named Dave who attended one of my sessions in Brooklyn. He played in college and was still active in New York City's high-level men's leagues, though he felt like he had never reached his full potential as a player. "TJ, I've been shouting—and shouted at—on the soccer field my whole life," he said to me a few weeks after the session. "I swear, I used to hear 'Man on!' in my sleep after some matches. I never realized what a distraction it was until I took away the noise and focused instead on playing 'eyes up' ball. It's like I've been eating soup with a fork all this time and you walked over and handed me a spoon. Through repetitive practice, Vision Training has taught me to stay connected with the ball. The game slows down because I'm calm, relaxed, and have more options. I'm able to see and make informed decisions while still maintaining possession of the ball."

I hope you'll indulge me here in one more extended testimonial because it shows the extent to which the people who benefit the most from Vision Training are often the biggest skeptics in the beginning. The story involves my good friend Glenn Crooks. If you follow soccer in the U.S., you no doubt know Glenn's name. The guy's a legend, with a career that spans more than five decades, including fourteen years as the head coach of Rutgers University's Division I women's soccer program. These days, fans of Major League Soccer know him as the national radio voice of New York City FC, and he also hosts several popular podcasts—*The Coaching Academy*, *On Frame*, and *Soccer in the City*.

I first met Glenn in the early 1980s, when we were both starting out in the game. He was a cub sports reporter at a local radio station in New Jersey and I was cutting my teeth as a high school assistant soccer coach and summer camp director.

One of my early ventures was starting a tournament in Jefferson Township, New Jersey, that within a few years was attracting many of the biggest men's clubs in the metro NY/NJ area, like the Metuchen Rovers and the famed Dover Strikers. I thought it would be cool to get some local media coverage. Glenn had a growing interest in soccer, so he agreed to come down and cover some of the action, including the championship match between my own club, Jefferson Township SC, and Dover, played on a patchy grass pitch before a few hundred fans, most of them immigrants from places like Mexico, South Africa, Costa Rica, Scotland, Germany, and Italy.

Glenn and I chatted a bit that weekend, then kept in touch in the ensuing years, as I continued down my soccer path, getting the Vision Training Soccer program in full swing, while building out my career as a college coach. Glenn's casual interest in soccer had developed into a full-blown passion, not to mention his full-time occupation. He had catapulted all the way to the collegiate level, starting with the women's program at LIU in 1997. The first-ever coach of the Lady Blackbirds, he developed the Long Island program from the ground up.

Glenn had a great reputation at LIU and in fact was instrumental in my taking over the men's program in 1999. For all the mutual respect we had for each other, he wasn't a big believer in Vision Training, at least not in the beginning. I recall the first time I mentioned it to him on a recruiting trip to Sweden during the summer after my arrival at LIU. We were having a rest after the red-eye flight from New York, fighting off jet lag, when I mentioned the concept. On the recruiting trip, we'd been talking about qualities to look for in players. Glenn mentioned things like speed, athleticism, bite, and finishing ability, all of which made sense. But they weren't the ones for me.

"Do they see the field and make smart decisions based on what they see?" I said.

"Well, sure, these are athletes," Glenn replied. "They have to be able to run and look around them."

"If they've been taught how to do it," I said, pushing back. "Effective vision isn't something you're born with. It's something you discover. That's what Vision Training is all about."

"Yeah, right!" said Glenn, with a condescending look.

Glenn would later joke that it was the jet lag that made him so dismissive, but whatever the cause, he wasn't interested in talking about Vision Training one minute longer. Over the course of the next few days, as he watched me interact with players and coaches on the trip, I could see his interest in Vision Training starting to grow.

We were on the return flight home, somewhere over the Atlantic, when Glenn turned to me and said, "Tell me more about this Vision Training."

"No way. I'm not going to tell you anything," I said, without a hint of humor, though I was smiling to myself.

"What do you mean?" Glenn asked, genuinely perplexed.

"Every time I've brought up Vision Training in the past, you've dumped all over it. So, no, I'm not going to tell you anything."

Glenn slunk back into his seat. After a few minutes, I started to chuckle.

"What?" Glenn said.

"I'm just messing with you, buddy," I said. "Let's get to work."

I pulled out my notepad and sketched out a few of my best intro-to-Vision-Training drills.

"In soccer, as in life, first memories have enormous influence over the formation of habits," I started. "When young players first touch a soccer ball, where do they look?"

"Down at the ground," Glenn answered.

"Exactly," I said. "So the first step is to break them of that habit and get them to look around, eyes wide open, scanning the field for information."

I walked him through a simple exercise I use to rewire my players' brains. With a ball at their feet, I have them look straight ahead and do simple movements—push the ball forward, pull it back, roll it side to side, and so on. As they become more comfortable with the ball, they make larger, faster movements, like dribbling laterally and switching directions. It's a simple drill that empowers players with the information needed to make quick, well-informed decisions. This is the first crucial step to begin building the habit of looking up and around.

"Once they're empowered on their own," I continued, "the next step is to get your players to connect with others." I sketched a second drill involving groups of fourteen to sixteen players in a forty-yard grid. At first, the goal is to scan and move within the grid, staying as far away from each other as possible; the key is finding the open space. Then they need to make eye contact with another player and switch positions at speed; now we're teaching recognition and validation. Then a ball is played into the grid and players have to scan and pass it around, earning points every time they look to the side or behind them before receiving the ball; now they're learning how to eliminate blind spots and achieving success through group connection. All of this is done without anyone shouting, clapping, or calling for the ball. We eliminate the noise. Athletes, dancers, writers, artists, they all perform their best when they're in the "flow state." When everything slows down and they are fully immersed, energized, and focused. On the other hand, noise is a distraction—it slows down your brain's ability to process information, and it destroys the flow.

"It's the same way in the game of life," I said. "When someone has blinders on, their field of vision is going to be narrow and they're going to miss out on so much information. As a result, their decisions are going to be narrow too. Only by opening their eyes, scanning, and shifting their lens will they have the capacity to gather relevant information and learn. As they learn, they change. And as they change, they grow."

The more I spoke, the more Glenn leaned into the whole philosophy of Vision Training. It was a breakthrough moment, the proverbial scales falling from his eyes. As we touched down at JFK airport, I told him I'd come to his first training session of the spring season. He couldn't wait to get started.

Fast-forward again, six months this time, to the end of the '99 season. The combination of Vision Training and talented new recruits had given the Lady Blackbirds their first winning season. Not only that, if they won their last game of the season, they would go through to the finals of the Northeast Conference Tournament, and have the opportunity to punch their ticket to the NCAA tournament. They did just that.

Glenn ended up writing a column in the New Jersey *Star-Ledger* about that game, and the impact Vision Training had had on his team throughout the season. To this day, the article is one of my favorite testimonials to the power of Vision Training. Here's an excerpt:

> With five minutes remaining in a scoreless match, our center back directed a pass to our striker, who approached the ball with her back to the goal as she looked over her right shoulder. Seeing a defender moving in fast, she eliminated the opponent by taking her first touch to the left. Her next touch was a 22-yard shot that settled into the back corner of the goal. We won that match and eventually the NEC championship. Not one teammate told our striker which way to turn to goal. She made the decision on her own by looking.

Glenn admitted in the article that he had his doubts at first about Vision Training. By the time his team lifted the NEC trophy in the fall of 1999, he was a true believer. As he put it, "A goal in vision training is to make 'looking around' a habit for each player . . . The most effective first-touch decision is made by the player receiving the ball, not by a player standing 20 yards away and yelling 'turn' or 'man on.' Remember, the speed of light (vision) 186,000 miles per second, is immensely faster than speed of sound (verbal) 1,000 feet per second."

Unfortunately for LIU, Glenn left the program the following year to take the reins at Rutgers, where he imparted the benefits of Vision Training to an elite crop of women players, including Jonelle Filigno, a standout on the Canadian National Team, and of course Carli Lloyd, whose fifty-five-yard wonder goal in the 2015 World Cup finals I talked about earlier. "It was a split second," Lloyd told reporters in her post-match interview. "Every single game I play I'm always checking to see where the goalkeeper is. She was really off her line."

The Lloyd story is a good one. But any time Glenn is asked about his favorite example of Vision Training, he goes to a player named Nicole, who he had at Rutgers around the same time as Carli. She didn't get a lot of playing time, in part because she never really got behind the Vision Training.

About a decade later, Nicole contacted Glenn out of the blue. She was living in Tennessee, where she worked as the director of a youth soccer club. She wanted to know if Glenn could send her some materials on Vision Training. "I remember how impactful it was at Rutgers, and I want to share it with my players," she told Glenn. Glenn sent the materials to her right away. And today, some of the best players in the country are coming out of Tennessee.

The people who end up getting the most out of Vision Training often start out as its biggest skeptics. You just have to get them to pick their heads up, look around, and see the possibilities.

The Second P: Process

Okay, back to the Five Ps. Even as the most perceptive players are taking five-plus looks every ten seconds, they need to analyze and abstract the data that's coming in. This is the process phase of the Five Ps and it paves the way for fast, adept decision-making. My players develop it through practice and repetition. It's about pattern recognition and knowing the likeliest outcome in any situation. (Another side note to coaches: Notice I didn't say pattern *repetition* just now, but rather *recognition*. In training, I don't use specific pattern drills, since they don't leave room for independent thinking and improvisation on the ball. Instead, attacking sessions are designed to empower players to improvise based on what they see. As the training progresses, I ask them to consider their options and make the most informed decision. Sessions are structured around small-sided games, and free play with specific coaching cues and performance objectives for players and the team to achieve.)

To demonstrate what I mean about pattern recognition, I like to share the story of Diego Maradona's goal against England in the semifinals of the 1986 World Cup—not the infamous "Hand of God" header, the second, far more impressive goal that came to be known as the "Goal of the Century." If you haven't seen it, you must go and find this extraordinary clip. The diminutive Argentine picks the ball up in midfield and quickly dances away from two English defenders. He then turns on the jets and dribbles the length of the right-hand flank, slaloming past three more defenders, before slotting the ball past the English goalkeeper, Peter Shilton. Eleven touches in eleven seconds that transcended the game. It's the ninth and tenth touch that I always talk to my players about. At that moment, Maradona was about fifteen yards from the goal and didn't have the best angle to shoot. He did, however, have two teammates drifting into the box and could have easily slipped the ball into the six-yard box for an easy tap-in.

One of those teammates was Jorge Valdano, who later recalled, "At first I went along with him out of a sense of responsibility, but then I realized I was just one more spectator." After the match, Maradona visited Valdano in the locker room and apologized for not passing the ball. He said he thought about laying it off, but as he approached the goal he remembered a similar situation against the English keeper from *seven years earlier*. He didn't score that time. But in that split second, while dribbling at full-speed on soccer's biggest stage, he was able to recall that information and this time beat Shilton by feinting left, juking right, and burying the ball with his left foot before getting absolutely pummeled by the English defender.

This is what processing data looks like at the highest level. The best players like Maradona build up vast databases of memories that they use to make smart, split-second decisions. Real life doesn't always call for such quick thinking. In fact, it often pays to be slow and deliberate in our sorting of information. The important thing is that the processing occurs. There are many ways to do this. I always encourage my students and players to keep a journal. The process of writing down your thoughts allows for self-discovery and will strengthen your memory.

Finding a mentor, regardless of what stage of life you're in, is another excellent way to process. Even meeting with a close friend once a week for a deliberate catch-up will get you to focus on the important things in your life. Whatever method you choose, be deliberate in your processing, especially in the beginning. The more you do it, the more automatic it will become, putting yourself in position to make the right decisions every time, without really even having to think about it.

The Third P: Plan

This is where strategy comes in. Once that player on the field has taken in the data and processed it, then it's time to come up with an action plan. Sometimes this planning happens in an instant—the defender is closing in hard, so it's either release the ball with a one-touch pass or spin out of trouble, as Maradona did so effectively in the goal of the century when he first received the ball at midfield. In a different situation, there may be time to take a touch and dribble into open space, or perhaps deliver a penetrating pass behind the defensive line to a teammate making a diagonal run.

Good planning is all about thorough preparation. As I shared with you earlier, the "flow state" is a crucial benefit when applying Vision Training and the Five Ps. Specifically, Mihaly Csikszent-mihalyi, the so-called Father of Flow, in his landmark 1975 book, *Beyond Boredom and Anxiety*, examined the conditions that lead to peak performance in sports; his 1999 follow-up, *Flow in Sports: The Keys to Optimal Experiences and Performances*, co-authored with Su-san Jackson, is the absolute bible on the subject. While he identified various factors that help athletes get into the zone, preparation of mind and body run through them all. The total control that peak athletes feel, the transmission of time, the effortless movement, the loss of self-consciousness, none of these happen by chance. Rather, it's through countless hours of practice and preparation that we're able to achieve true states of flow.

I want to qualify that last statement by saying the practice must be mindful and deliberate. You've probably heard the old coaching adage, "How we practice is how we play." It's absolutely true. I can often tell by Wednesday what kind of a game my team is going to have on Saturday based on the quality of the training. Are players engaged and focused? Is there good communication? Are problems being identified and solved in real time? If the answer is yes, yes, and yes, I know we're in good shape. If not, I need to figure out what's wrong with *my* planning and make the necessary adjustments.

Visualization (which I'll talk about at length later in the book) is another vital component of the planning phase. Many professional athletes embrace it. Think of the MLB baseball pitcher Max Scher-zer, famous for taking bullpen sessions in his full uniform to better visualize game situations. Or Olympic gold medalist Lindsey Vonn, who liked to visualize every frame of a downhill race. "By the time I get to the start gate, I've run that race one hundred times already in my head, picturing how I'll take the turns," she once said in an interview. This is visualization at its most extreme. Even small applications will make you more successful in life—picturing and seeing yourself giving a successful presentation, for example, or imagining having an impactful meeting with a new manager for the first time, or anticipating how joyful you'll feel listening to and mentoring a close friend or colleague. It's all about being ready for life's moments by thinking them through in advance.

The Fourth P: Perform

We are now in the execution phase. A plan is in place, one based on a thorough processing of information that's been taken in with the widest possible lens. It's "go" time. Here again it's about being in the zone. Sports psychologists talk about the importance of mental execution to the process. This is the ability to mentally perform at high and consistent levels during athletic competitions or other situations requiring focus and situational response. We've all seen athletes or teams who are outmatched physically by their opponents, but end up winning because of their superior ability to execute.

Several factors impact performance, and they all tie into Vision Training and the Five Ps paradigm. There's the ability to drown out distractions and process information at a rapid rate. Maybe you've heard of the Stroop effect, defined as the delay in reaction time between congruent and incongruent stimuli. The best example is a test involving a mismatch between words and colors, for example the word "red" printed with blue ink and the word "blue" printed with yellow ink. Respondents who take this version of the Stroop test are asked to say the color of the word, not what the word says. They're much more prone to answer incorrectly when the word does not match the color of ink it is printed with. But those who are able to maintain high focus speeds can zero in on the right informational cue. Improving your focus speed, and thereby executing at the highest level, comes back to maintaining a wide, bright lens.

Think of the soccer player on the field who receives the ball with a defender closing down fast. Does he play a one-touch pass to a supporting teammate? Does he elude the defender and find the open space? Or does he freeze, because he's receiving an overload of information—commands from coaches and fans, warnings of "man on" from his teammates, which is preventing him from identifying the correct decision? Another important acronym of Vision Training that comes into play here is the Three Ss, short for "shield, scan, spin." Watch the best players in the world, from Lionel Messi to Luka Modrić, and you'll see the method in action throughout every match. It's critical to maintaining possession and finding offensive opportunities. The first S, shield, occurs when the player with the ball uses "eyes up" awareness to recognize a closing defender and positions their body between them and the ball. Next, they use the second S, scan, to find the outlet. Then comes the final S, with the player spinning away from pressure and into the open, flowing space. Achieving that flow state on the soccer pitch is only possible when players are empowered to gather early, real-time information and process it to independently make the right decisions.

The same goes for life beyond the pitch. Perhaps you're in a meeting at work and need to synthesize conflicting sets of information to guide the team to the right decision. The better you perceive, process, and plan, the easier it will be to perform in these high-pressure moments. Or think about navigating personal relationships. Your ability to gather information, both verbal and nonverbal, will make you a more compassionate and effective parent, partner, friend, and so on. The pattern recognition that comes with this process will improve your situational awareness, empowering you to make quick, smart decisions.

Now let's switch gears and talk about anxiety management, another key component of mental execution. There are countless stories of professional athletes who let their anxiety get the best of them and suffered a serious case of the yips as a result. How about Rory McIlroy at the 2011 Masters? On the Saturday of the tournament, he shot a 70 to finish at 12 under par with a 4-stroke lead. But on the next and final day, he came back with an 80, dropping him to fourth place. Or I'll never forget Andy Cole missing sitter after sitter for Manchester United during the final match of the 1994 Premier League season, denying his club the championship.

Managing anxiety in the context of the Five Ps comes back to decision-making. Decisiveness is one of the biggest predictors of success. When I'm scouting for a top player on a recruiting trip, this is one of the things I look for the most. The player who is constantly looking to their coach or teammates for direction, or who seems to be second-guessing every decision they make, is a red flag in my book. Because it means they are going to be racked by anxiety when the inevitable mistake occurs. Instead, I search for players who are clearly in command of their own intuition, who are able to make on-the-fly adjustments as needed through the course of a competition, and who are not afraid to make a play that carries some element of risk. These are all signs of a player whose ability to perceive, process, and plan has set them up for high levels of performance.

of their top coaches to do a super clinic here in Helsinki. Every year it's the same old stuff.' He said to tell you this is the best thing he's ever seen in his life."

"Wow," was about all I could manage. I was breathless! I always believed in the transformative power Vision Training had back home, but this was next-level validation. That gentleman forgot more about the game than I've ever learned, and he loved it. I couldn't help but wonder what would happen if every player in the U.S. trained this way.

And that's not even the best of it.

Cut to seven years later. I was in Southern California for the United Soccer Coaches Convention, an annual event that draws coaches, trainers, and instructors from all over the world. One night I was at the hotel bar and was introduced to a Finnish gentleman, a young guy in his thirties named Pekka, who it turns out was the director of coaching education for the Finnish Football Federation.

"Yeah, I've been to Finland before," I told him. "Your country is beautiful."

"Thank you," he said. "What took you there?"

So I told him all about Vision Training—head on a swivel, gathering information, planning, problem-solving, innovating—and about the course I put on in his country many years earlier.

He looked at me closely and paused for a long moment and then he said, "This is very interesting and fascinating. We have been wondering for many years now why so many of the most creative youth players in our country seem to be coming from Turku. Now I know."

Now you know too. With the Five Ps at your disposal, you're ready to become the best version of yourself. To do that, there are a few more secrets I want to let you in on.

Chapter Five

LOOK, LISTEN, LEARN

The Three Ls of Vision Training

From the Five Ps to the Three Ls. The ability to look, listen, and learn ties in so directly to the Five Ps that it makes sense to talk about them in order. This also gives me a chance to expand on the importance of Vision Training. I know I've written a lot so far about the need to eliminate noise on the soccer field (no shouting for the ball or "joystick" coaching when your teammates are on the ball), the same way you need to cut out unnecessary distractions in real life to be able to focus on what matters most. But this doesn't mean I expect my players or students to turn off their ears. Just the opposite—I want them to engage all their senses as they take in as much information as possible. When it comes to Vision Training for Life, attentive listening is one of the most important strategies of all.

I learned this lesson in the best possible way about two decades ago, following a chance encounter with one of my biggest personal heroes.

Get on the Right Bus

As part of the Philosophy of Coaching course I taught at Long Island University-Brooklyn, we examined different coaching styles from the world of college and professional sports. We'd start by looking at coach-centric examples like Bill Belichick, the furrow-browed NFL boss who led the New England Patriots with an iron fist to nine Super Bowls in twenty years, winning six of them. Or Bobby Knight, Indiana University's hotheaded basketball coach who demanded total control of his Hoosiers (and later Red Raiders when he moved to Texas Tech) both on and off the court.

Then I'd introduce my students to more player-centric coaches, like Phil Jackson, spiritual guru of the Los Angeles Lakers, known for giving his players curated book lists to read in their off time. Or Alex Ferguson, whose success at the helm of Manchester United was due in large part to his mastery of "man management," or his ability to meet players where they were, not where he wanted them to be. Or Carlo Ancelotti, who I had the pleasure of meeting at an international leadership conference in New York City. At one point in our conversation, I asked him what his biggest coaching mistake was and what he learned from it. His answer: trying to change the way Andrea Pirlo, the brilliant Italian midfielder, played to suit Ancelotti's needs when he coached him at AC Milan. It didn't work and it taught him the importance of giving players the freedom to let their uniqueness shine.

It won't surprise you to hear that I've always aligned myself with the player-centric approach. Jackson and Ferguson both have my utmost respect, but in my mind, one stands above us all for his flawless execution of the coaching style: Duke basketball's legendary Hall of Fame coach, Mike Krzyzewski, known to most simply as Coach K. Throughout his four-decade career at Duke, Coach K consistently empowered his players to make their own decisions. Instead of calling a time-out during big end-of-game moments, more often than not he'd trust his players to figure things out on the court. That's exactly in line with the core principles of Vision Training—creating a framework for players to succeed by making smart, well-informed decisions *on their own*.

I also admired Coach K's style of communication, which was based on validation. My students and I would watch post-game interviews, parsing his every word. Invariably, he'd start by complimenting his opponent, no matter how badly the Blue Devils had just beaten them. "We had a hard time breaking them down in the beginning because they were coming at us so hard with the high press," he might say. Or he'd single out the play of the opposition's scrappy point guard or dynamic power forward. There was always such specificity to the kudos, rather than pat praise for the opposition. Then Coach K would bring it around to his players, again giving a very pointed analysis of what they did right. "I'm on their bus; they're not on my bus," he liked to say, forever giving full credit for Duke's success to the players on the court. The line comes from a piece of advice his mother gave him before he headed off to high school. "Get on the right bus with the right people and your bus will go to places that you could never get to alone," she told him. He obviously took his mother's words to heart. To be the winningest coach in NCAA history and still have so much humility is just awesome to me.

So, yes, I'm a huge Coach K fan. You can imagine my excitement when, back in 2003, I was at a Broadway performance of *Les Misérables*, and seated a few rows in front of me was none other than Mike Krzyzewski. I've met a reasonable number of famous folks in my life, but I was nervous as can be to meet my all-time favorite coach. Through the whole of the first act I was thinking to myself, "You have to go say hello during intermission. This is a once-in-a-lifetime opportunity, TJ." The lights finally came up and I did just that.

"Coach K, just wanted to introduce myself and say a quick hello," I said. "I'm a soccer coach, but I've followed your career from the beginning and I really respect what you bring to the game. I've tried to apply many of the same ideas into my own methods."

I was ready to leave it at that, but Coach K immediately engaged me in conversation, asking questions about my own coaching journey. Where did I coach? How was the program? How was I feeling about the upcoming season? The guy was genuinely interested!

"So, are you enjoying the show?" he asked, once the coaching chitchat came to an end.

"I'm loving it," I answered. "I'm actually here to see a good friend who's one of the leads."

"No kidding," he said. "Which one?"

"The actor playing Javert is Chris Innvar, one of my oldest friends in the world," I explained. It was true, Chris and I were roommates out of college and went into the wine importing business together before the acting bug took him in another direction. Talk about persistence—this guy has it in spades, but that's a story for another time.

"That's amazing!" Coach K cried. "I'm here with my wife and three daughters, and my youngest daughter Jamie's favorite character is Javert."

"You think she'd like to meet him?" I asked.

Coach K called over to his daughter and put the question to her. Jamie basically said there wasn't anyone in the world that she'd like to meet more. So we went back to our respective seats for the second act and agreed to meet after the show, outside the 47th Street side exit that all the actors use.

As we were waiting there, I introduced Coach K and his family to my wife, Donna, and we all made more small talk. After a few minutes, Chris exited the theater. Like me, he's a huge Coach K fan, so I'd already decided I was going to play a little trick on him. I walked over to greet him, carefully shielding Coach K from view with my body.

"Hey, Chris, great show—you were incredible," I said. "Listen, I want you to say a quick hello to an old friend of mine." I then opened my body and there was Chris standing face-to-face with the Duke legend.

"Oh my God!" he screamed with the full force of his stage-trained diaphragm. "It's Coach K!" The youngest Krzyzewski might have been excited to meet a real-life Javert, but that was nothing compared to Chris's elation in front of Coach K. We all enjoyed a good long laugh on one of those picture-perfect summer nights in New York City.

The love fest ultimately came to an end, and it was time to say goodbye. As I went to shake Coach K's hand, he said this to me: "Anytime you want to come to a game, just let me know. I'd love to have you and Donna be my guest."

I want to pause right there. As I've explained, Coach K was already an idol because of his incredible player-centric coaching style. But in that moment, the simple fact that he remembered my wife's name taught me one of the greatest lessons of all: the immeasurable impact of close listening and validation.

But wait, it gets even better. Several months later, I took Coach K up on his offer, putting a request in with his secretary for tickets to a game. A few days went by, then a week, and I figured he never got the message, or was too busy to deal with it. Hey, we're all human, right? But then one night Donna and I came home to a message flashing on the answering machine. I hit PLAY.

"Hello, TJ," he began. "It's Mike Krzyzewski . . . from Duke." I loved that he felt the need for that qualifier! He continued, "I am so sorry that I haven't gotten back to you yet. I've been busy re-cruiting for the last four weeks on the road. This is a very important season for us so I've been laser focused on the incoming class. But I would absolutely love to have you and Donna come to our game against Villanova. Please contact my secretary, and she'll make all the arrangements."

Three months had gone by since our random meeting in a Broad-way theater, and Coach K still remembered my wife's name. I know Donna felt about ten feet tall hearing her name come out of Coach's mouth on our answering machine. Heck, I felt ten feet tall. I vowed then and there that I would strive hard and do my best to remember every person's name that I met. This was the beginning of the in-corporation of close listening and leaning into the Vision Training methodology.

Mastering the Three Ls

I think we can all agree the human brain is a busy place. Science tells us the average brain processes eleven million bits of informa-tion every second. Our conscious minds, however, can only handle forty or fifty bits of information per second. That's not a very high retention rate! Neurologists have also found that, of the information that is recognized, only 1 percent is remembered. In other words, 99 percent of our conscious life literally passes us by.

In his superb book *The Happiness Advantage*, Shawn Achor shows the effect of this by referencing a famous psychology experiment in which two hundred volunteers were asked to watch a portion of a basketball game on tape. About twenty-five seconds into the video, a man in a full gorilla suit walks slowly across the court. Afterward, the volunteers were asked a series of questions. Which team scored more points? How many passes did you count? Which player committed the most fouls? And lastly: Did you notice anything unusual about the game? Believe it or not, 46 percent of the volunteers completely missed the gorilla. Many of them refused to believe they could have overseen something so obvious and insisted on watching the video again. Of course, now that they knew to look for the gorilla, it was impossible to miss.

In the last chapter, I talked about how the Five Ps enable you to expand your perspective and gather more data. The Three Ls are about zeroing in on the best information so that you can form meaningful, lasting connections with others. The more connections you make, the more elevated your life will be. Remember how Coach K's mom put it: get on the bus with the right people and your bus will go to places that you could never get to alone.

Remembering people's names is one of the simplest ways to form connections, though I know so many people struggle with it. I used to be that way myself. That night at *Les Misérables* with Coach K, as we all departed, I had no idea what his wife and daughters were called, because I hadn't developed the skill yet. In the years since, I've honed it to the point where I consistently remember a person's name. I see how powerful it is in creating a framework of respect and recognition. As Dale Carnegie famously put it, "A person's name is to him or her the sweetest and most important sound in any language." Saying someone's name confers instant validation.

The secret to remembering names is repetition. The first time you meet someone new, repeat their name early and often. In my Vision Training for Life workshops, I demonstrate this by engaging with someone in the crowd I've never met before. After a minute or two of chatting, I'll ask the audience how many times they think I used the person's name. They usually guess two, three, maybe four times, when in fact I'll have said the person's name eight times or more. The technique is so effective because every time you say the person's name, your brain forms a new memory of them, and the myelin sheath that contributes to memory formation and recall in our brains becomes stronger.

Remembering people's names is a good first step in using active listening to form meaningful connections. How do you take the Three Ls to the next level? In my Philosophy of Coaching class, I created an assignment called the Positivity Project. The terms were simple: over the course of a three-week period, my students had to figure out a way to make a meaningful connection with as many strangers as possible. Keep in mind, the class meets in Brooklyn, New York, not exactly the small talk capital of the world. And a lot of the students were from tiny towns, including villages in other countries. So the thought of engaging with strangers was terrifying for some. Others were introverts who preferred to keep to themselves. Then there were the handful of hardened cynics who thought the project was just plain dumb.

Monica, a student in the class and star softball player for Long Island University, fell solidly in the camp of poo-pooers. "This project is dumb, TJ," she said to me flatly. Monica was not one for mincing words.

"Give it a try, Monica," I responded. "What's the worst that could happen?"

Three weeks later, we were back in class and I asked for volunteers to share their results of the Positivity Project. Guess whose hand went up first?

"Go ahead, Monica," I said with a smile.

"Right, so I chose the lady at the bagel shop," Monica began excitedly. "I'm in there at least three times a week for a year, we've never so much as made eye contact. But I know I have to do this assignment, so I notice she's rocking a new hairstyle. 'Nice haircut,' I said to her. She looks up at me with this big smile and says 'thank you.' I don't know, maybe she was having a bad day before, but it really made her happy. A few days later I'm back in the shop wearing my softball sweatshirt. 'You play softball?' the lady asks. I tell her I do, then she says her daughter plays softball. She's a sophomore in high school, so the bagel lady wants to know about LIU's program. I told her about it, and also about the summer camp we run for younger players. I think her daughter might actually sign up for it. Now every time I go to the shop, this lady I knew nothing about before starts making my bagel without me asking and we chat for a few minutes. It's pretty cool."

"That's more than pretty cool, Monica," I said. "That's transformative. For you, for the bagel lady, for the bagel lady's daughter. And all it took was one compliment over a haircut."

This is the Three Ls in action. Instead of staring at her phone while in line at the bagel store, the way most of us do these days, she picked her head up and noticed her server's new haircut. By engaging her with a small compliment, she created space for a connection to form. In that space, Monica and the bagel lady were able to learn something about each other and the connection deepened. By sharing the experience with the rest of the class, the ripple effect of the positive interaction spread even further. Through decades of Vision Training, I've seen this phenomenon on the field, in the locker room, and in life. There will be team-wide resistance at first, but then one or two players will have a breakthrough. Their teammates will pick up on it and start to emulate and soon everyone on the squad is playing smart, eyes-up ball. Human connectivity is the best kind of contagion.

Empathy and the Three Ls

The creation of space is so critical to both Vision Training and Vision Training for Life. On the field, it's about making intelligent and purposeful runs to open up the defense or creating just enough separation between yourself and the defender to get a shot off. In life, the creation of space is often about slowing down and being in the moment, really listening as the other person talks, giving them your undivided attention. It's about searching for the meaning of their words and not getting caught up in the details. It's hard work! You want to interrupt and jump in with your own thoughts. Or maybe you want the conversation to end so you can check your phone or go grab lunch. The antidote to these urges and impulses comes down to one thing: empathy. To become proficient in the Three Ls, and in turn the Five Ps, you must be able to put yourself in the other person's shoes.

As a coach and educator, I'm in a position to practice empathy every day. One example stands out in my mind. This was maybe five years into my time as the head coach at LIU. I'd built the program into enough of a success to the point where we were drawing talented players from all over the world. One of them was a Swedish defender named Jonas Stigh. With his 6'2" frame, he was built like a Viking, an imposing presence who quickly established himself as one of the best players in the league. He was a true leader, too, confident and focused, so much so that I decided to make him our captain.

After a successful campaign that year, Jonas returned for his senior season. Hopes were running high for him and for the team. But seemingly overnight, Jonas came undone. It was preseason training when he started showing up late for practice just about every day. Through reviewing his progress reports, I saw that his grades were slipping, whereas before he consistently received high marks. At training, he was often combative with his teammates. I would address it with him and his behavior would improve for a day or so, but then he would fall down again. My assistant coaches were imploring me to take stronger action.

"We have to suspend him, TJ," one of them said to me one afternoon, following a particularly nasty outburst from Jonas on the training pitch.

"I don't want to do that," I responded. "At least not yet."

Later that night I spoke with my wife, Donna, who was a trained counselor.

"TJ, there is something going on with Jonas," she said. "When someone acts out in this way, there's always a reason behind it. Instead of disciplining Jonas, you need to listen closely to understand what's going on inside."

The next day I called Jonas into my office. It was more like an oversized closet, with just enough room for my desk and a small sofa.

As Jonas entered, we both literally had to turn our bodies sideways so he could squeeze past and take a seat on the sofa.

"Jonas, this behavior of late is so unlike you," I began. "I want to understand what's going on."

"What are you talking about, Coach?" he answered, immediately going on the defensive. "I had two assists against Sacred Heart the other day. I'm one of the leading scorers on the team and I'm our center back."

"I'm not talking about your stats, Jonas," I said. "It's the other stuff. Your grades, your getting in scrapes with the guys. It's not like you. The Jonas that I know is passionate and cares about his teammates and cares about his schoolwork."

He started to resist further but then I could see the fight disappear. It was like watching a balloon lose air.

"Coach, I'm having a tough time," he admitted.

"What's going on?" I asked.

"I honestly don't know," he said, with a softness in his voice I'd never heard before. "I'm not sleeping. I'm not eating. I'm anxious, sad, and really down. And I just don't know why."

At that point I continued to go softer and become more empathetic with Jonas. I asked him to share more of what he'd been feeling. He was a very private person, plus as our captain and leader I knew he felt the need to project strength and confidence. But slowly, he allowed himself to admit that he was hurting and in need of help.

"I'm not sure how to sort this out," he said.

"Well, can we start by getting some counseling for you?" I asked.

"Yeah, Coach, I think I'd like to do that," he answered.

"Can I call right now?" I asked.

"Would you, please?"

I picked up the phone, dialed the number for on-campus

counseling, and handed him the receiver. He set up an appointment for the following day. I gave him a big hug and sent him on his way. Over the course of the next few weeks and months, Jonas made steady improvements. One therapy session didn't take away the stress and anxiety, but he began developing the necessary coping tools and strategies.

By the middle of the season, Jonas was operating at full capacity. I won't say he was back to his old self, because a new Jonas had formed. Still strong and confident, but with a deeper self-understanding that made him an even better player and person. That turned out to be a breakout year for the program. In the finals of the NEC tournament, against our arch rivals Fairleigh Dickinson University, we won a corner kick in a 1–1 draw with under a minute to play. Our center mid drove the ball deep into the box. As it drifted toward the far post, Jonas sprang into the air above the defense and nodded it into the back of the net. We punched our ticket to the NCAA tournament with the win and Jonas was named tournament MVP.

After the match, I remember wondering what might have happened if I had come down hard on Jonas six months earlier. What if I had suspended him from the team, from our soccer family, rather than leaning on empathy to get to the root of his problem? His downward spiral would have likely continued, resulting in his removal from the team and possible school suspension. We most certainly wouldn't have been headed to the NCAA tournament. But far more importantly, Jonas might not have gotten the help he needed. Instead, he finished up a successful career at LIU, on the field and in the classroom. He stayed in the U.S., married a wonderful woman named Daniela, had two beautiful children, and is now a soccer coach himself in New Jersey, where he no doubt practices empathy in his shaping of young players.

I like the phrase "practicing empathy," because it stresses the fact that empathy, rather than being an immutable trait, is something that we can learn and develop over time. In their book, *Humanity on a Tightrope*, psychologist Robert Ornstein and biologist Paul Ehrlich talk about the need for humanity to widen its scope of empathy. "The need to expand our connections and cooperation with strangers is essential right now," they write. "All of us, citizens of every nation, are now in the same family, are now in the same boat, walking the same tightrope, like it or not." The message might sound a little apocalyptic, but the underlying sentiment is spot on. We are on this earth to form human connections with others. Empathy is the surest way to get there.

Becoming the Best Sports Parent Through the Three Ls

I now want to switch gears into practical advice for using empathy and the Three Ls to lead a more positive life. As the section heading suggests, this advice is aimed directly at parents of athletes. However, anyone in a leadership role will benefit from it. First, a story from my own early days as a parent.

My youngest daughter, Caroline, played for a youth travel team near the New Jersey shore town where my kids grew up. It was a great group of girls—some more experienced than others, but a tight-knit crew that supported one another and had a lot of fun. One of her teammates was a special talent named Carina (not her real name). At that age, it's still a lot about athleticism and physical attributes, and Carina could outrun and overpower every other player on the field. But she was such a genuinely nice kid that she played most of the game in third gear, so as not to crush the opposition too badly. I'll never forget the time that, in a rare moment of competitive zeal, she ripped a volley from ten yards out right into the gut of the goalkeeper, who promptly crumbled to the ground. After catching her breath, the keeper was fine, but Carina was inconsolable for the remainder of the match with the thought that she'd hurt another player. That's the kind of kid she was.

Now let me tell you about her parents. Her father used to pace the sideline like a lion, his eyes trained on Carina, following her every move. He didn't say much, but his body language spoke volumes, none of it good. Carina's mom was the screamer. You could hear her throughout the match, shouting commands at Carina, ranting at the referee, and even criticizing players on the other team. It was a sight to behold.

One day, Caroline and I were pulling out of the parking lot of the field after one of her matches. It was a well-played match that showcased the talent of two wonderful youth teams. I don't recall what the score of the game was, or whether we won or lost. In the pickup truck in front of us were Carina and her dad. Through the rear window of the cab, we could see Carina's dad tearing into his daughter. Clearly, his silent sideline demeanor ended the moment he was alone with Carina. Caroline and I watched as he pointed an angry finger at Carina. Now it was Carina's body language that spoke volumes, as she leaned heavily against the passenger door, desperate to get as far away from her father as possible.

"I feel so sorry for Carina," Caroline said. "She played great today."

"She sure did," I said. The pickup truck darted out of the lot in one direction and we drove off in the other. "What about you, Caroline?" I asked. "How did you feel out there?"

Caroline spent the next few minutes breaking down her performance—what went right, what went wrong, and what she would look to do differently the next time out. I told her I was proud of her. The score of the game didn't come up once.

—

For over twenty years I taught a college class in sports science at Long Island University. I spent a lot of time talking about youth sports, since they have such a massive impact on childhood development. It was always the most popular section of the course, because it resonated so deeply with my students, most of whom played competitive sports at one time in their life; many were still doing so at the Division I college level. I could see the flicker of recognition in their eyes as the coursework touched on something they'd experienced as kids. The classes were so popular that I began offering a workshop for parents titled How to Best Guide Your Child Through Youth Sports.

I always start the workshop by asking the parents to list the top five reasons they want their kids to participate in sports. Over the years, I've probably put the question to thousands of parents. Some common answers include things like "to build character," "to make them more competitive," and "to teach them how to win." They might mention the social benefits of team sports or the importance of physical fitness. But the dominant theme by far is around this idea of raising a winner.

I'll then pull up a national survey of twenty thousand children nationwide, which asked the same question of them. Why do you participate in sports? The survey lists the top ten responses. Care to guess what's number one on the list? If you're thinking to yourself "to have fun," give yourself a pat on the back. That's exactly it. To have fun! Now guess where "to win" falls. If you guessed "number ten," you might be able to skip this chapter altogether.

Most parents, though, even those with high emotional intelligence, put more emphasis on winning and not enough on having fun. The fact is evident in the attrition rate in youth sports. One report in the *Sports Business Journal* estimates that 70 to 80 percent of youth athletes will drop out of sports by the time they reach high school. The number one reason kids quit? It's no longer fun!

I get it. We all live in a competitive society where the importance of getting ahead (i.e., winning) is hammered into us from the earliest age. For a handful of athletes, this drill sergeant approach works out—think of Tiger Woods swinging a golf club at the age of three under his father's watchful eye. Or Andre Agassi, who wrote about his father's militant tactics in his 2009 memoir, *Open*: "Nothing sends my father into a rage like hitting a ball into the net. He foams at the mouth ... My arm feels like it's going to fall off. I want to ask: How much longer, Pops? But I don't ask. I hit as hard as I can, then slightly harder."

For every Tiger and Andre, there are thousands upon thousands of kids who leave the game because the pressure to win takes all the fun out of it. I think back to Carina, sitting in the cab of that pickup truck. Whatever burgeoning soccer passion she might have had was being squeezed out of her with every jab into the air of her father's finger.

There is a better way and it's built around the principles of Vision Training for Life. Whether you want to become a more transformational leader in your own life or you want to help your child become a transformational player in their respective sport, the process is the same. It's all about creating a framework and a set of conditions where success is possible. For parents looking to navigate the choppy waters of youth sports, I've boiled the teachings of Vision Training into the following Dos and Don'ts.

I can't promise that if you follow these rules your child will play Division I sports, or even crack the starting lineup of their high school team. But I can guarantee that, barring other external forces, they will stay in the game, they will contribute to building a healthy culture, and they will be happier, more whole-hearted individuals as a result. As Mauricio Cienfuegos, the great Salvadoran pro player and former star of the Los Angeles Galaxy, once put it, "If your daughter likes soccer, art, or another sport, support her in what she does. The most important thing is for your children to be happy and to do what they love."

TJ's Dos and Don'ts of Parenting Through Youth Sports

Don't shout from the sidelines. You sometimes hear this referred to as joystick parenting—moms and dads who try to control their kids' actions on the field, court, or rink by barking instructions. "Shoot the ball!" "Make the tackle!" "Pass the puck!" This kind of behavior happens all over the world, but it's particularly common in the U.S., with its outsized emphasis on winning. I once had a player who said she couldn't concentrate on the field because her mom was too loud on the sideline. Can you imagine?

As I discuss throughout the book, the problem with joystick parenting (or coaching, for that matter) is that it develops players who can't think on their own, because they're constantly waiting for someone to tell them what to do. Your goal as a parent should be the same as that of their coach: to create the necessary space for your child to independently identify and make the most informed and best decisions. Of course, you can be at the games, cheering them on, but any joystick parenting is going to have the opposite effect from what you intend, impeding their development, rather than promoting it.

Do show positive encouragement. Remember, kids participate in youth sports to have fun and feel worthy. Any feedback you give your child should be geared toward those goals. Keep the cheering lighthearted—tone and body language are just as important here as the words out of your mouth. Also, as you're watching the action, make a mental note of a play or two where your child does something positive. It could be a clean pass or the execution of a new skill they've been working on in practice. You don't need to bombard them right after the game with the observation (a simple "good job out there!" is best at that moment). Later in the afternoon, or even the next day, find the chance to recognize the achievement. "Hey, I was just thinking about that through ball you played Charlie yesterday," you might say. Or, "It was great how you recovered from that double fault in the first set with back-to-back aces." Or, "I loved your effort and how you were first to so many 50-50 balls." Or, "Kudos to your attitude and how well you responded after giving up that first goal." The point is to encourage your child and help them understand how sports is a way for them to feel more competent and successful in their lives.

Don't ask if they won or lost. Remember, winning is last on the list of reasons why kids want to play sports. I can recall being at a youth game with an old friend, watching his kid's team play. They ended up losing the match pretty badly. Within a few minutes of being released by the coach, the kids had forgotten all about the defeat and moved on to some other spontaneous activity. This annoyed my friend. "Don't they even care that they lost?" he seethed. I reminded him that the purpose of youth sports is to help kids experience joy and self-expression. The fact that the team wasn't dwelling on the loss was a sign of mental wellness, not a lack of competitive drive. He accepted my point, grudgingly. As adults, we must never forget that our whole conception of winning and losing is different from that of our kids—unless we make them hyperaware (and mentally unhealthy) by constantly harping on score lines and win-loss records.

Do ask how they played. Self-understanding is essential to personal fulfillment, and it's critical in the development of young athletes too. That's why the best question you can ask after a game is always, "How did you play?" It encourages your child to analyze their performance and look for growth opportunities, the way my daughter Caroline would on our car rides home together. As part of my research for this book, I asked Caroline to share more about the experience. "This question [How did you play?] immediately took any pressure or expectation away from winning," she wrote in an email to me, from her home in Savannah, Georgia. "When I carpooled home with other players after games, most parents focused on the result of the game and their child's performance. As a result, these players seemed more anxious and nervous to mess up for fear of disappointing their parents." She went on to describe how players whose parents focused on winning were unable to see the big picture, including their child's personal development and that of the team. "I was never nervous after games to talk to you," she wrote, "even if I played poorly, because I knew it was an opportunity to grow." Those words from Caroline mean more to me than any game won or goal scored ever could.

Don't oversubscribe your kid. Another major contributor to mental burnout is excessive playing and practice. Watch out for early warning signs, which include a sudden disinterest in the sport, a lack of pride in playing, and an unusual focus on aches and pains. Nip the burnout in the bud by scheduling time-outs away from the sport. Or try to get them interested in another activity. There's a lot of debate around single-sport versus multisport athletes. While sports specialization can lead to higher levels of early success, it also increases the chance of burnout. Picking up a second sport, even casually, will help your child keep up the passion for their primary sport. It can also prevent injury by developing different muscles and motor skills.

Do encourage free, unstructured play. There are many reasons U.S. men's soccer has not yet been able to succeed on the world stage (emphasis on "men's" there; our women are consistently successful!). But perhaps the biggest is the lack of pickup soccer here, unlike other parts of the world, where the game is literally played in the streets. In his riveting 2018 book, *The Away Game: The Epic Search for Soccer's Next Superstars*, Sebastian Abbot delves into the impact of unstructured play on game intelligence. He references a 2012 study of the English Premier League, which found that the players with the highest soccer IQs played one and a half times more pickup as kids. This type of training, Abbot writes, "creates the opportunity for players to experiment with different skills and tactics in an unstructured environment, leading to better anticipation and decision making."

The culture in the U.S. is starting to shift, with more unstructured play happening across all sports. If pickup games exist in your community, encourage your child to participate on a regular basis. And if there aren't any, help your kid start one up. Depending on their age, getting out there with them for a little mixed-age pickup is a great way to create stimulation and excitement, while getting a quick run in yourself.

Don't be an interference. Screaming their heads off from the sidelines is the most obvious example, but there are more subtle ways parents interfere with their child's development. Bribery, for instance. I've known parents who pay their kid money for every goal they score. This is an example of extrinsic motivation, in which the child performs an activity to earn a reward or avoid some form of punishment (like their parent's wrath). It's the opposite of intrinsic motivation, whereby they perform the activity for the simple pleasure and fulfillment it brings. Parents can also be an interference by trying to act as a second coach. Anytime I work with a youth team, I always start the season by meeting with the parents. My message is simple: it's crucial that you don't give information to your child, because it's probably not going to align perfectly with what I'm telling them. And I'm going to lose that battle every time, since a child is always going to listen to their parents over their coach.

Do be an influence. Your job as the parent is not to bribe them with rewards or fill their heads with too much information. You are there to help your child learn how to stay composed and relaxed. Athletes who are afraid to make mistakes never learn to play freely and imaginatively. As I discussed earlier, it starts by getting them to focus on the process—asking "How did you play?" not "Did you win?" The more you pose reflective and introspective questions, the more they will learn to problem-solve on their own. And this skill will transfer to all aspects of their lives, from the classroom to personal relationships, up through their professional careers and their own family-rearing.

Do help them practice selflessness. The final, and perhaps biggest, quality you can help cultivate in your child athlete is selflessness. Besides getting them to analyze their own performance, encourage them to find positives in their teammates. The willingness and ability to learn from other talented players (when the natural instinct in our hypercompetitive world is to feel threatened or to criticize them) is another hallmark of a well-balanced youth athlete, one who will stay in the game into adulthood and reap enormous personal rewards as a result.

Life is full of distractions. It is full of noise. We are all moving a million miles a minute. At every stage in life, it is so easy to get swept up in the chaos. The Three Ls are all about slowing the game down in order to find purpose within ourselves and meaningful connections with those around us. Coach K did this when he made a mental note of my wife's name. The softball player from my class at Long Island University did it when she took a moment to compliment a stranger's new hairstyle. And every parent does it when they bite their tongue on the sideline and let their child find the game on their own.

As you become more accustomed to refreshing your lens on a regular basis, I hope you will also get more comfortable with the Three Ls, using them to block out the noise and find the magic, both big and small, that is happening all around you.

Chapter Six

DISCOVER THE JOY OF THE GAME

The morning of October 3, 2018, was a glorious one in Brooklyn. Beneath a brilliant blue sky, the low sun cast long shadows across the training fields at LIU.

"I'm grateful for this beautiful day," our center back Huib said.

"I'm thankful for the chance to train hard with great friends," our keeper Cole added.

"I'm grateful because I absolutely know we're gonna keep rolling," our striker Rasmus shouted, eliciting a chorus of woo-hoos and yeehaws from his teammates.

Every training session of ours starts with this ritual—the gratitude circle, as I call it. The team circles up and gives thanks and shout-outs to whatever it is we're feeling grateful for at that moment. It's the way to get a positive mindset before hitting the pitch.

This gratitude circle was especially meaningful because just a couple hours earlier the president of the university had dropped an absolute bomb on the entire LIU sports community. For months, rumors of massive cutbacks had been circulating, including the possible dismantling of the entire Division I sports program at LIU's Brooklyn campus—though no one really believed that could actually happen because the Blackbirds were such a revered institution at the school. The men's soccer program, in particular, had an illustrious tradition dating back to the 1930s. We had the very first Hermann Trophy (college soccer's equivalent to the Heisman) winner back in 1967 in Dov Markus, the Russian-born striker who one season scored thirty-five goals in fourteen games, setting an NCAA record. When Major League Soccer held its first draft in 1996, LIU alumni were chosen among the most from any other college or university. And recently the program was only getting better, including three trips to the conference championship in the last four years.

At 9 o'clock that morning, all the head coaches across the entire program—soccer, basketball, tennis, golf, baseball, softball, and so on—had been summoned to the fourth floor of the athletic department. As we took our seats, a gentleman no one had ever seen before slowly stood up. We soon learned that he was the vice president of LIU's Post campus and he was there to inform us that the sports programs from the two schools would be merging into one. It still galls me how he made it sound like this was the greatest news in the world.

"I don't understand, which campus gets the program?" one of our coaches asked from the back of the room.

"We'll be taking full advantage of Post's tremendous facilities," the man responded, a classic non-answer.

"Wait, isn't Post Division II?" someone else asked.

"That's correct," the man answered.

"So what happens to the Blackbirds?" we all asked.

"The Blackbirds will no longer be known as the Blackbirds," the man responded, a slight edge creeping into his voice. "The Blackbirds are no more."

The finality of his words hung over the room. It was like getting kicked in the gut.

At that moment, in another meeting room on campus, hundreds of LIU student athletes, including my soccer guys, were simultaneously getting the same horrific news. It was a real travesty. Think about all these students who had chosen LIU because they wanted to study in New York City, specifically Brooklyn, with a host of career opportunities and be a part of an elite Division I program. The administration really did them wrong.

As I made my way back to my office after the announcement, I thought about my cousin George Hayduchok, one of my best friends, actually more like a brother. He and his wife, Nadine, had been there for me in a big way when I was going through my divorce. I recalled the way he always preached the importance of controlling the things you can control and letting go of the things you can't. The Blackbirds would soon be no more. No amount of hand-wringing or letter writing or organized protest was going to change that.

But we still had this season. Its fate was 100 percent in our control and no one could take that away from us. That's the message I opened with as we circled up later that morning. Most of the guys still had a look of shock and disbelief on their faces.

"I'm grateful that we're here with our family and that we have these next few weeks together," I started. "Let's be sure to live each moment deeply and intentionally. We are not going to permit anyone or anything to impact the success of our program. This season is ours and it can't be taken away. I'm grateful for that."

Even as the world around us was coming undone, the vibe in the gratitude circle that morning was positive and resolute. Other LIU sports programs on both campuses began to fall apart within days of the announcement. There were stories of players quitting and moving on, trying to navigate the next steps in their journey, and games being canceled. The men's soccer program persevered and moved forward because we had worked so hard at creating a culture of gratitude and positivity around it. The work at building a healthy, inclusive, and sustainable program had started years ago and it would carry us through this challenge.

This team had done the reading group that I'll talk about in chapter ten. As part of the exercise, we had created a team ethos, basically a list of values that defined the character and spirit of the program. We began the list with integrity, but gratitude and positivity soon followed. We made the commitment to use the fundamentals of Vision Training (perceive, process, listen, learn, etc.) to seek out the bright side, the goodness in what we had.

It sounds simple, yet I can't emphasize enough how vital gratitude is to mental health. As I sit here writing, I can honestly tell you that I haven't had a bad day in eight years because of my daily affirmations in gratitude. The practice begins the moment I open my eyes, when I consciously and deliberately thank the Lord for blessing me with another day on this planet. Next I do a brief meditation, scanning and appreciating each part of my body—lungs, veins, heart, brain. Finally, I think about three things that happened the day before that I'm most thankful for. It might be a warm embrace from an old friend, or how the players at one of my sessions improved their vision and decision-making, or simply a delicious meal

I was fortunate enough to enjoy. The whole ritual takes less than ten minutes and it sets me up for a positive, joyous, and peaceful day.

There is a vast and growing body of research out there explaining the many benefits of gratitude. In one study, Dr. Martin E. P. Seligman, a psychologist at the University of Pennsylvania and a pioneer in this field, used 411 volunteers to test the impact of positive psychology interventions, the term for setting yourself up for positive thinking. To do so, he had his experimental group send letters of gratitude to people in their lives whose act of kindness they had never before recognized. The control group did nothing. At the end of the week, the letter writers showed a tremendous increase in happiness scores, and those mental benefits lasted a full month. Other studies show how gratitude has physical benefits, too, everything from improved cardiovascular health to better sleep.

Practicing gratitude and positivity can even improve your vision. It's true! Mood and mindset actually change how our visual cortex processes information. In an experiment conducted by researchers at the University of Toronto, volunteers were primed for either positivity or negativity and then shown a series of pictures. Those who were put into a negative mindset missed substantial parts of the picture, while those who were in a positive headspace saw everything. Positive thinking actually expands our peripheral line of vision.

Words of Gratitude

LIU's players and coaches were the most devastated by the dissolution of our Division I sports program in Brooklyn. But the many decades' worth of Blackbird alumni weren't far behind in their feelings of loss and betrayal. Part of the beauty of playing at the elite college level is it enters you into a tight-knit community that thrives long after graduation. Being a member of Blackbird Nation meant something big to so many men and women, even as their lives moved far beyond LIU's Brooklyn campus.

Within days of the October 2018 announcement, an online petition protesting the move had garnered more than 4,000 signatures, many of them Blackbird alumni. A Facebook group called LIU Blackbirds Forever quickly swelled to more than 1,500 members. "It's been real, Brooklyn!" one member commented. "To the place that I've called home for the last seven years, thank you. Thank you for helping me grow personally and professionally, thank you for the fellow Blackbirds that became friends and family, thank you for the memories."

Even my old mentor Norman Schwartz, who roamed the LIU Brooklyn campus in the 1950s, added a comment, saying that "being a 50+ year alum it is a very sad time for me to say goodbye to the Blackbirds and this wonderful esprit de corps, coaches from all disciplines and leadership in all areas of education."

Walking home in the days after the bomb drop, along Brooklyn's Smith Street, with its eclectic mix of hipster bars, chic restaurants, and old-world mom-and-pop shops, I was struck by the extent to which gratitude was the dominant emotion coming from our alumni. Sure, they were mad as heck. But they were also incredibly grateful to have worn the Blackbird shield. Their immense feelings of gratitude sustained them. That gave me an idea.

As soon as I got home, I pulled out my laptop and sent an email to several of my former players who I was still in close contact with, asking them each to write a note to the current team describing what it means to have been a Blackbird. My initial plan was to read one of the notes before each of our remaining matches. As it happened, there wasn't nearly enough soccer left for all the letters that poured in, but I knew I would find a way to share every sentiment.

Our first match following the admin's bomb-drop was against a scrappy, talented side from Central Connecticut State. We were riding a five-game winning streak, but of course the tenor of the season had shifted. I walked into the locker room, asked the guys to circle up, and pulled out a folded sheet of paper from my pocket.

"Anyone know the name Jukka Lehto?" I asked. A few hands shot up.

"Finnish guy, right?" my right back said. "Played up top."

"Damn right," I said. "Four-year starter. Led the squad with twelve points his senior year in 2008. One of the nicest and toughest players I ever coached." I then told the guys about my alumni letter-writing project.

"Jukka was one of the first to respond," I explained. "Here's what he had to say."

I handed his letter to one of our captains, the Norwegian Marius Koss, and asked him to read it. Marius was a quiet, soft-spoken young man. His uncle was Johann Olav Koss, the five-time gold medalist Olympic speed skating champion and *Sports Illustrated*'s 1994 Sportsman of the Year. As he began to speak, I observed as everyone became still and gently leaned forward to listen closely.

Jukka really was a special kid—total hardness on the field, total humility off, and that was evident from the opening line of his letter.

"First off, thank you for the honor of being able to write to you guys," he said. He then shared a few details from his life (settled in Mexico City with his wife and son, good job, etc.) and explained that he'd been following the 2018 season closely.

Then he wrote this:

"My second son, Leevi, was born on February 20, 2018, with

a complex heart disorder called transposition of great arteries. He died soon after during open heart surgery. The reason I'm sharing this story with you is that at the time when my son was being operated on, the guys I reached out to and who gave me their support were my fellow Blackbirds ... What I want to express to you guys is that life after college is hard and full of challenges. The chance that you as a team have is special. You are the last Blackbirds and you have been given the opportunity to win the last NEC title. Life after this season will be very different. But the memories and friends from LIU will be there for life! The most important thing is what do you do right NOW!!!"

Marius handed back Jukka's letter. I folded it and put it back in my pocket, and let the silence hang over the room. No interpretation of Jukka's words was needed. The guys understood.

"All right, let's bring it in," I said. "Team on three!"

The guys took the field and played ninety minutes of fluid, dynamic soccer, meeting defensive challenges head-on and hunting second balls with unrelenting passion. In the 65th minute, our center midfielder, Daniel Quiros Herrero, intercepted the ball and played it forward to our attacker, Romario Guscott, who juked their keeper and buried the empty netter. The winning streak went to six.

The letter-reading ritual went on for the rest of the season. Before our next match against Sacred Heart, the team heard from Ryan Vanderkin, Class of 2007, who told them to "enjoy every bus ride, every practice, every joke, every win and every person. AND BY GOD ... ENJOY EVERY GOAL!!" 3–2 overtime win for the good guys.

Next up, Mount St. Mary's, and words of gratitude from Ricardo M. Ordain, a member of the 2005 NEC Championship soccer team. "Playing in Brooklyn was an experience I will never forget.

I learned the power of faith and of believing. It's very important that you all remain focused on your individual and team goals. Have a vision of yourself achieving your goals and work hard for it. Don't allow anything or anyone to take that vision away from you." 2–1 overtime win for the good guys.

Week after week it continued, all the way to the NEC finals on November 11, 2018. The final letter came from Andrew Zarick, who captained our 2004 championship squad and went on to work for Verizon, heading up its innovations lab. He recounted a few tales from his playing days, then made light of the fact that he never thought he'd be the old guy telling war stories to the young guard.

"As players we'd joke that the old guys would tell the same stories every year, because they did!" he wrote. "I always think back to what I would have done differently as a student or as a player. There is one thing that I always come back to: Be conscious of the fact that the guys in this room and the people at this school are the people who you're creating lasting memories with. These memories will literally last a lifetime. They're also the memories that you, too, will be telling year after year. Why not make them incredible, and play some sexy football while you're at it?"

Fifteen minutes later, the Blackbirds were ready to take the field at LIU for the last time, facing Bryant University in the NEC championship match. Rasmus Hansen, one of our top players and leading scorer, came up to me as he got on the pitch. "Coach, there's absolutely no way we're losing this game," he said. "I just want you to know that."

Forty days had passed since the administration's bombshell. It could have been a period of anger, mourning, and loss. Instead, it was one of the most uplifting experiences of my life, because through the power of positivity, gratitude, and persistence, we refused to let anyone or anything get in the way of our destiny.

Our guys were on fire from the opening whistle. Eight minutes in, we went ahead on a nifty near post first time finish by our striker Zach Peterson. The score remained 1–0 until the second half, at which point we really poured it on. It was forty-five minutes of pure, passionate Blackbirds ball. The second goal came from Zach once again, as he curled a left-footed shot into the far corner, just out of the goalkeeper's reach. The third goal saw Rasmus on a 55-yard, 1v1 counter taking on Bryant's top defender and then driving the ball with pace just inside the far post. The final goal on that iconic pitch came from our bulldog Chris Solbakken, who, after winning the ball, burst into the box and buried it under the diving goalkeeper's hands. Final score: 4–0, good guys! The last soccer team to play in Brooklyn went out the only way we knew how: as champions.

How to Be Grateful

I share that story of the Blackbirds' final season because it shows how the deliberate act of practicing gratitude is truly transformative. It's why I believe so strongly in the importance of keeping some kind of gratitude journal. My final three years at LIU I even incorporated the practice into the Philosophy of Coaching course that I taught. Initially, I opened each class with the same gratitude circle I did with my soccer guys, going around the class and having each student share something that they were thankful for that day.

The ritual brought such a positive energy and joy to the class that I decided to broaden it out into the journal that counted for 25 percent of the class grade. Each day students had to write three things in the journal. First, the gratitude piece—three things they were happy about at that moment. Second, they had to list an academic goal for the day, like finishing a chapter in a book or putting in for extra credit. Then a physical goal—for example, walking ten thousand steps or hitting the gym. Finally, there was the social component, which I defined simply as small acts of kindness that made the world a better place, like picking up a piece of litter from the streets or engaging a stranger in friendly conversation.

At the end of each semester, students completed an anonymous questionnaire designed to measure happiness. My hope was that a third of them would see an uptick in happiness, maybe half if I was lucky. I kept careful stats over the three years. Would you believe that 83 percent of students were more joyful at the end of the four-month semester? In some cases it was more than 90 percent! That includes my final spring semester in 2019. Most of my students were athletes, so they were still reeling from the sad news about LIU's sports program. Their lives had been turned upside down. And yet, after four months of conscious gratitude and goal setting, they were in a happier state of mind. They had rewired their brains and refreshed their lens and decided that extraneous events happening around them would not affect their happiness. That, my friends, is the power of gratitude in action. It's the equivalent of lifting your eyes up in soccer, scanning the field, and seeing the many options and opportunities that are all around you.

What are some other ways to bring gratitude into your life? For me, being ever mindful of any hardship and loss that I've experienced in the past helps maintain a grateful outlook. Robert Emmons, a professor of psychology at the University of California, Davis, the world's leading scientific expert on gratitude, calls this "remembering the bad." He writes, "When you remember how difficult life used to be and how far you have come, you set up an explicit contrast in your mind, and this contrast is fertile ground for gratefulness."

In my case, remembering the bad takes the form of counting blessings, because I've had so many close encounters with death—eight to be exact, and that's not even counting the nail that took my eye out when I was twelve. These are even closer brushes with death, like inches away from nearly being decapitated by a steel cable when I worked a summer job in college at a sand and stone quarry in New Jersey. Or the double bypass open heart surgery I had at the age of forty-four. Or the time a commercial airplane I was flying on with my LIU team to California had a technical malfunction and plummeted into a nosedive, ten-thousand-plus feet in a matter of seconds, before the pilot miraculously overcame the instrument malfunction and saved our lives. Hopefully you don't have the same catalog of near-death experiences to draw on, but everyone goes through hard times during their life. Remembering these times can help keep you in a current state of gratitude.

I also encourage people to refresh their lens by finding something new and beautiful that they hadn't noticed before. It may be as simple as the color of leaves on a tree when the sun hits it a certain way, a hearty welcome from a friendly neighborhood dog on your daily walk, a red poppy flower in the neighborhood garden, or a warm smile from a stranger. As part of my research for this book, I reached out to hundreds of former students and players, asking them how Vision Training has impacted their life. One of my favorite responses came from JM (John Michael) Richards, a former Bard College squash player from Los Angeles.

"Part of the beauty of Vision Training is its simplicity," he wrote. "I do not keep my eyes low on the sidewalk, but keep them observant and humble, encountering the world as I pass by. When I walk with friends, they often are taken [a]back by the things I point out: 'Did you see that bird? Did you notice that its wings were two different colors?' They often do not notice these things because their field is not as expansive as mine. Through the use of the 5 Ps, I have been able to fill myself with the beautiful, the unexpected, the obscure, and the tangible in all aspects of my life. Like the birds that usually go unnoticed, these became a part of my working experience . . . I encounter great people—and great lessons—daily. The '5 Ps' not only make the world more accessible, they make one more open to the chance encounters, friends, and strangers on the street that all play a role in our field of vision."

The final key to finding gratitude has to do with your interactions with other people. Every new encounter is an opportunity to show appreciation. Seek out ways that you can be helpful to others. We all have the ability to lift and inspire people who come into our day, for example by validating their ideas or offering support or perhaps advice. Always express your gratitude in person. When someone goes above and beyond, make sure to verbally let them know that you appreciate them. On that note, pay attention to language. As Emmons writes, "Grateful people have a particular linguistic style that uses the language of gifts, givers, blessings, blessed, fortune, fortunate, and abundance. In gratitude, you should not focus on how inherently good you are, but rather on the inherently good things that others have done on your behalf." One very simple example of this is saying "I appreciate you" to others and not "I appreciate it."

Find ways that you can go above and beyond by showing kindness to others. Offer to make a coffee run at work. Keep your **eyes up** for opportunities to hold a door open, help someone carry extra boxes, move chairs, and so on. Seek out and find the best in others. Focus on the goodness of the folks in your orbit, including family, friends, and coworkers. When they do something positive, let them know. This will help rewire your brain to see more of the positive qualities in people. Listening deeply is also a form of bringing energy and validating others.

Finally, bring positive energy to every conversation, and don't take away energy by complaining or focusing on the negative. No one wants to be around negative people. They bring us down and sap our energy. Always remember this: seeing positive equals being positive.

The Power of Synchronicity

Okay, time to get mystical.

Since I adhere to Christianity as my faith, there's plenty of spirituality in my life. But you could also call me pantheistic, which posits that the universe is interconnected by all gods in all religions. My parents were Ukrainian Orthodox, and my grandfather, whom I worshipped, was a priest, so I was raised going to church and worshipping the Holy Trinity of the Father, the Son, and the Holy Spirit. But I've embraced all aspects of every religion throughout my life, from Buddhism to Judaism. In the end, I consider myself deeply spiritual.

If there's a religion to Vision Training, it's synchronicity, or the belief that higher powers are all around us, if only we're willing to let them in. Only by living life with our eyes up and open wide are we able to fully seize on this extraordinary power.

Shortly after graduating from college, I went out to Los Angeles with my old college roommate, Mike Buday. One night we went to a little comedy club in town, one frequented by famous comedians who liked to try out their material in front of smaller audiences before taking it on the road. This was the early '80s, so it was names like Eddie Murphy and Sam Kinison and Ellen DeGeneres. But there was only one person I had in mind.

"Maybe Robin Williams will show up," I said to Mike, with a huge grin as we jumped in his car and raced to the club. I should mention that we were a couple of cash-strapped twentysomethings, so instead of buying tickets, we decided to sneak in through the side entrance of the adjoining restaurant. Well, we must have had more courage than smarts because within two minutes the manager came over and tossed us from the club. We decided to grab a beer from the restaurant before heading back home.

We were halfway through our lagers, licking our wounds over the recent indignity, when who do I see approaching the side entrance to the comedy hall—Robin Williams! Before entering the club, he took a detour into the bathroom. I jumped from my seat and made a beeline for the men's room. It was cramped quarters, with barely room for the urinal, toilet, and a small dingy sink. Robin was in the stall when I walked in, so I took my time pretending to do my business and began to wash my hands. Eventually he emerged from the stall.

"Robin Williams, what a pleasure to see you!" I said warmly. "My name is TJ and I'm a huge fan." He was cordial enough, especially given that we were squeezed into a tiny restroom in downtown L.A.

"Hey, I just wanted to let you know that I thought you were amazing in *Moscow on the Hudson*," I added, referring to the 1984 film in which Williams plays a Soviet-era circus musician who defects during a tour of the States. "My parents are Ukrainian and we spoke it in the house. I took a year of Russian language studies and you absolutely nailed it. I have to tell you, your accent was just perfect."

"That's very kind of you," Williams responded with a huge smile on his face. "I took a three-month intensive language immersion course with the goal of speaking fluently. This is the first time that anyone has ever noticed."

As we made our way out of the bathroom, he asked if I was there to see the show. Just as I was about to respond, the manager who had thrown us out a few minutes earlier passed through the swinging doors to the club.

"Hi, Bill," Williams said. He then turned to me, wrapped his arm around my shoulder, and with a huge grin on his face exclaimed, "Do me a favor and find a good seat for my friend. I invited him here tonight to see my show." The next thing you know, the scarlet-faced manager stepped off to the side and quickly escorted me to a seat in the front row.

A minute later I saw Mike cautiously peek his head through the doors. I waved him over to our seats, the best ones in the house. We had a hearty laugh over our good fortune and an even better one when Williams took the stage to try out his new material directly in front of us.

It's No Coincidence

One might hear that story about Robin Williams and chalk it up to simple coincidence. At the time, I even did so myself. But as the years passed and I became more immersed in Vision Training, in particular the power of maintaining a wide, open lens on the world, chance encounters and unexplained phenomena started happening with amazing regularity, so much so that I started keeping a record of them in what I came to call my synchronicity journal.

Some of the moments are minor. I'd be sitting at a traffic light and my mind would wander to one of my daughters or to an old friend and a second later my phone would ping with a text message from that very person. Others were more extraordinary. Take the journal entry for August 26, 2016. I was in Albany, New York, for LIU's first game of the season, staying at a hotel downtown with the rest of the team. Standing in line at the breakfast buffet, I felt a chill, the intense presence of someone from my past staring at me. I scanned the room but didn't see any familiar faces. So I got my breakfast and took a seat at a table. A moment later I looked up and there in front of me was Dr. George Pappas, my next-door neighbor from my childhood home in New Jersey, whom I hadn't seen in over a decade.

"George, what the heck are you doing here!" I shouted.

"My oldest daughter is at the Albany pharmacy school," he explained. "We always stay at this hotel when we visit. I saw a few guys wearing LIU soccer shirts. I knew that you coached somewhere out on Long Island, so on a whim I asked if any of them had ever heard your name. 'Yeah, he's sitting right over there having breakfast,' one of them said."

We had a nice laugh over the good fortune, caught up on our lives, and exchanged phone numbers. When I got back to my room, I realized that the bus wouldn't depart for another ninety minutes. I called up George to see if he wanted to connect some more.

"Sure, what floor are you on?" George asked.

I told him the third floor, which he laughed at, saying he, too, was on the third floor.

"What room?" he asked.

"Room 324," I answered.

He told me to open my door. I obliged and, sure enough, to the amazement of us both, there was George standing in the doorway to the next room over with his cell phone to his ear and a huge smile on his face.

"Next-door neighbors again," he said, and we laughed some more.

The more of these experiences I had, the more I realized they were not the product of mere coincidence, but instead were a function of my openness to the magic of the universe. I compare it to the maxim in sports that great players get lucky. Of course, luck has nothing to do with it. Rather, these players have incredible natural abilities combined with exceptional vision that allows them to see and seize on opportunities that other players don't. Who can forget Tiger Woods sinking an impossible chip shot on the 16th hole at the 2005 Masters Tournament? It's been called the luckiest golf shot ever, when in fact Tiger simply read the green and the lay of the ball better than anyone else possibly could.

This is what happens with synchronicity when you live life with your eyes up and your lens wide, open, and deep. Sheer coincidence plays no part. It's about getting yourself into a positive, receptive mindset, one in which you're in a position to take advantage of the synchronicity that's happening all around us.

Richard Wiseman, a psychologist at the University of Hertfordshire, conducted a ten-year study into the nature of luck and found that, for the most part, people make their own good and bad fortune and, furthermore, that it's possible to enhance the amount of luck you encounter throughout your life. In one study, 69 percent of high school and college students said that major career decisions were influenced by chance encounters. Those students whose brains were primed to expect favorable outcomes in life were able to capitalize on the encounters. For the others, the opportunities passed them by.

As Wiseman explains, "Lucky people generate their own good fortune via four basic principles. They are skilled at creating and noticing chance opportunities, make lucky decisions by listening to their intuition, create self-fulfilling prophecies, via positive expectations, and adopt a resilient attitude that transforms bad luck into good."

What do those four principles remind you of? If you're thinking to yourself, "the Five Ps," you just made my day (and yes, you better believe I can feel it!). When we Perceive, we notice opportunities. When we Process, we listen to intuition. When we Plan, we make smart, well-informed decisions that only seem lucky. When we Perform, we create self-fulfilling prophecies. And when we Persist, we adopt a resilient attitude that transforms bad luck into good. It's all right there, using the Five Ps to find synchronicity and spark joy in your life through spontaneous connection with others.

As with gratitude, there is a growing body of science-based research into the power of synchronicity. A book I've handed out over the years is called *Connecting with Coincidence* by Bernard Beitman, a psychiatrist, visiting professor at the University of Virginia, and founding director of The Coincidence Project, which encourages the use of synchronicity and serendipity in everyday life.

Beitman opens his book with a story about Carl Jung, the Swiss psychologist and psychiatrist and father of analytic psychology. One day Jung was riding the train to his home in Zurich when he was seized by the terrifying premonition of a person drowning. When he arrived home he learned that his grandson had nearly drowned right around the time of his vision. To describe this and other strange events he experienced throughout his life, Jung invented the word "synchronicity."

Beitman's own seminal experience with synchronicity was more tragic. It happened around 11 PM one night at his home in San Francisco. As he was getting ready for bed, he suddenly started choking, even though he hadn't eaten anything. It was fifteen minutes before he could swallow and breathe normally. The next day, Beitman received a call from his brother saying his father had died at his home on the East Coast after choking on his own blood. It had happened around 2 AM, precisely the time Beitman had his phantom choking episode.

The first half of *Connecting with Coincidence* shows how synchronicity pervades every aspect of our lives. It guides our search for romantic partners, our formation of friendships, the maintenance of physical and mental health, and even the generation of wealth. Beitman then moves into ways to make these life-changing coincidences happen in your life. Over the years, I've taken many of these ideas and pulled them through the extruder of Vision Training Soccer and Vision Training for Life. Here are the main takeaways from that process—my tips for harnessing the power of synchronicity.

Tip #1: Be a Believer

Spirituality has paved the way for synchronicity throughout my adult life. My belief in a higher power also enables me to believe in the usefulness of synchronicity. After decades of practice, it's now reached a point where synchronicity is an expected part of my everyday life. Beitman's term for people like me is "coinciders," or those who "more fluidly than others make connections between what goes on in their minds and the events in their environment." Beitman developed a tool called the Weird Coincidence Scale, which involves rating how frequently you experience common coincidences. Some examples include: "I think of calling someone only to have that person unexpectedly call me" and "I am introduced to people who unexpectedly further my work/career/education." After decades of believing, my score is off the charts. Yours needs to be as well.

I know this can feel like a leap of faith, especially for the highly rational-minded. I've talked about the skepticism that many players and coaches have when they first learn about Vision Training Soccer. Then they go through a few drills, their performance improves, the blinders fall away, and all of a sudden they can't imagine playing the game any other way. It's the same thing with synchronicity. Believe in its power and you will be constantly rewarded by it.

Tip #2: Increase Your Curiosity

An active mind is another requisite of synchronicity, and being curious is the best way to stir the brain waves. Beitman writes that "a coincidence begins with the improbable intersection of a particular thought with a similar event." Neither occurrence is likely for someone who sits on the couch all day watching television. People who move around a lot and have a natural curiosity about the world and others in it are much more likely to experience coincidences. There are ways to train your brain to become more curious, for example by taking a different route to work. I remember doing this one morning on my walk to LIU through my Brooklyn neighborhood. On a whim, I decided instead of walking my daily route down Smith, to travel down Court Street. A few blocks from campus I was shocked to run into an old friend from Sweden who I hadn't seen in years. He was in the U.S. touring colleges with his teenage daughter. We never would have connected if I wasn't curious to see another part of Brooklyn.

Tip #3: Prime for Positivity

Remember, good things come to those who expect them. Study after study shows how believing in positive change becomes a self-fulfilling prophecy. In a famous Harvard experiment conducted by the social psychologist Margaret Shih, a group of Asian women were given two math quizzes. The first time, they were primed to focus on the fact that they were women, a gender not as stereotypically good at math as men. The second time, they were primed to focus on their Asianness, stereotypically a group that excels at math. The women did much better in the second quiz. The questions hadn't changed, but their belief in their abilities had.

I have found in my life that a willingness to talk about synchronicity with family, friends, and colleagues (especially those who I trust are receptive to the theory) is a way to maintain a growth mindset around it. The more you talk about it, the more insight you'll get, both from yourself and the person you're sharing with. "Coincidences are more like signposts than directives," Beitman writes. They need to be pondered and discussed and interpreted. Sharing the experiences with others is one of the best ways to do this. I also encourage you to start a synchronicity journal, which could just be a section of your gratitude journal. The act of writing down moments of synchronicity from your life will train your brain to let more of them in.

Tip #4: Listen Up

Remember the Three Ls: look, listen, learn. Moving through life with your head on a swivel and being a good listener will open up synchronistic opportunities. Here's an example. Every summer, since 1981, I run a few weeks of Vision Training soccer camps in Pennsylvania and New Jersey with my partner Len Bilous. The camps are in the afternoon and evening, so I like to spend my mornings at a coffee shop getting work done. This summer, I was tapping away at my laptop when a mother and daughter, who looked to be in her late teens, walked in and sat at the table next to mine. I noticed the girl was wearing a soccer shirt. During a lull in their conversation I made eye contact and asked about the shirt.

"Yeah, I play for Kutztown college," she said. "I'm home for the summer."

"That's wonderful," I told her, then peppered her with a few more questions about her experience.

"Are you a coach?" the mom asked. I gave her the quick spiel, including about the Vision Training camps, then turned back to the daughter.

"Who runs the program at Kutztown college?" I inquired.

"Erik Burstein is the coach," she said.

"No kidding!" I responded. "Would you believe I coached Erik many years ago when he was just a teenager? It must be twenty years since I saw him last. I'm so happy he's doing well." We ended up going to the soccer page on her college website and looking at pictures. The wheels of synchrony were turning, and they were doing so because I did three things: I noticed the daughter's shirt (Look), I asked a question (Listen), and I gave space to the conversation (Learn).

But wait, I haven't even gotten to the good part. After we chatted for a few more minutes, the mom and daughter said goodbye. I turned back to my laptop. Twenty minutes later, I received a text from Len. He was at the soccer store that he owns just over the border in Pennsylvania. Here's what the text said: "Erik Burstein says hello. He was just in the store buying new boots." I was buzzing the rest of the day. That's synchronicity.

Tip #5: Stay Brave

It took some chutzpah to follow Robin Williams into the bathroom all those years ago, the same way I had to muster up the courage to approach Coach K at the Broadway production of *Les Misérables*. With Williams, my understanding of synchronicity hadn't taken shape yet, but I still knew the opportunity was a special one.

Just as with Vision Training, seizing on synchronicity requires quick, decisive thinking. As Beitman writes, "Coincidences are created by matches between the swirling contents of our minds and the swirling images and sounds of our circumstances. Each of these can move quickly. Develop a nimble attention, ready to seize the moment."

Ultimately, it comes back to the last of the Five Ps: Persistence. As mystical as it seems, synchronicity requires practice and persistence, just like any worthwhile pursuit.

When Gratitude and Synchronicity Collide

If you're familiar with college soccer, you'll know that our capture of the NEC Championship in 2018 meant we automatically qualified for the NCAA Division I tournament. So what happened next? Did the magical ride continue?

A week after our romp over Bryant in the conference finals, we traveled to Morgantown, West Virginia, to take on the #18 ranked Mountaineers. We were the underdogs for sure, but we'd basically been playing with house money all season, so we had nothing to lose, which was evident from the opening whistle to everyone on hand that frigid night.

Rasmus Hansen, our stud senior midfielder, netted two goals in the first ten minutes. The Mountaineers didn't know what hit them. We had them on the back foot for so much of the first half. But then they equalized on two quick goals of their own, though the second was on a controversial play where their forward was clearly offside. Not only that, he practically tackled our keeper, causing him to lose the handle on the ball.

The momentum shifted and the weather went from bad to worse, with a fresh layer of icy snow covering the field as we started the second half. Our opponents went ahead in the 75th minute and then iced it with another goal a few minutes later. That was it. The final flight of the Blackbirds. Though of course the memories live on in all of us.

Now for the synchronicity. A few years after the match, I was at a coach's conference in Boston and ended up sharing a room with a guy who was at the WVU match. I need to protect his identity here because at one point in our conversation he said this to me, "Anytime the Mountaineers played a big game at home, the referee always seemed to be in their pocket." I thought back to my final post-match interview that November night. After taking a bunch of questions, I was making my way back to the locker room when the NCAA representative who was there overseeing the contest stopped me in the hallway.

"I can't believe how gracious you were just then," she said. "I went down to the referee's locker room at halftime and ripped him a new one for missing that call. I am deeply sorry for you and your team but I can promise you he will not be assigned to any further matches."

"Well, I don't know if you had to do that," I said with a smile. "But I appreciate the kind words."

When I think back on that day and all the weight it carried—the Blackbirds' last match after eighty-three seasons, my final day at the helm of a program I'd built over two decades—it's amazing the lightness I feel. I'm not bitter about the referee's non-call because, among the many things you can't control in this world, officiating is high on the list. I'm sorry for my guys that we lost, but the overarching feeling I have for them is pride.

That's what a mindset centered on gratitude and synchronicity will do. It lets you see the best in yourself and the world around you. It allows you to form deep, meaningful connections that last a lifetime. It helps you delight in the magic of the universe. It brings joy to every moment.

During the post-match interview, a reporter had asked me to reflect on the season.

"It's been a remarkable season," I said without hesitation, then thanked him for posing the thoughtful question. "We had a nine-game winning streak at one point. The university is going through some hard changes, which we found out about in the middle of the season. The guys stuck together and they believed in each other. We often talk about family and how teams are families. Some of them are dysfunctional families and some are healthy families. This was the healthiest family I've ever coached in twenty years."

I'm forever grateful for that.

Chapter Seven

PLAY THE GAME
THE RIGHT WAY

A re you sure you even want to coach here anymore?" the man in a slick Armani suit asked. It was the vice president of LIU's Post campus, the same one who hours earlier had delivered the news that the school's NCAA Division I program in Brooklyn would merge with the school's Division II program, with all the outdoor sports happening out at Post. He was now meeting one-on-one, for fifteen whole minutes, with the head coaches from every program, asking the same question to each of us, probably in the same dismissive tone.

Did I even want to coach here anymore? Gee, let me think. LIU Brooklyn had been my home for the past twenty years. We'd built the program into a perennial conference powerhouse, with trips to the final four playoffs the last six seasons in a row, culminating with two championships. In the classroom, our teams posted equally impressive results, making the academic national top 20 for team GPA every year I was at LIU, often beating the likes of Princeton, Stanford, and Harvard. Twice we had the number one team GPA in the entire nation. Did I mention that we were in the middle of a five-game winning streak and we would finish the season with the best overall record in more than twenty-seven years?

I let the man's question hang in silence for a few seconds. I often do this in my conversations with people to create room to think and process. But I'll admit it, in this instance I just wanted the guy to squirm. It was working. With every passing second, he became more and more agitated, clearing his throat and tapping his pen anxiously on the table.

"I guess that's something I'll have to think about," I said finally, then stood up and walked out of the room. As I made my way back to my office, I knew there was nothing to think about. It was clear from the way he asked the question that TJ Kostecky was not part of LIU's game plan moving forward. Sure enough, a few weeks later, they offered me the assistant coach position, with the top job going to someone far less experienced. Talk about adding insult to injury.

No matter, I had already moved on in my mind. Which begged the question, What's next? We all have inflection points throughout our lives, some big, some small, but always our lives ebb and flow. These moments of transition are a perfect opportunity to shift and refocus your lens. They're a time for introspection and assessment when your Five Ps should be buzzing. That's the state of mind I was in as I made the mental break from LIU and began contemplating my next chapter in life.

The more deeply I considered my life, the more I knew that the next station I arrived at had to place a high value on ethics and integrity. In the Principles of Philosophy and Coaching course that I taught at LIU, I devoted an entire section to these ideals, since sport is an area where they're best expressed, going all the way back to the original Olympic Games, with its core values: "encourage effort," "preserve human dignity," and "develop harmony."

When played the right way, sports are guided by a set of moral principles and values that brings out the very best in humankind. It's called the spirit of the game, and some of my favorite examples come from soccer. There's the unwritten rule, for example, that if a player goes down with an injury, the opposing team when in possession will kick the ball out of bounds. Once play resumes, the team with the injured player automatically plays the ball back to the opposition. It's a simple etiquette that says so much about the integrity of the game.

One time in an Italian fourth division game between Fersina and Dro, it got even better. After a Fersina player became injured, Dro followed custom by kicking the ball out of bounds to stop play. Once play resumed, Fersina passed the ball back to the Dro goalie, who accidentally let it skip through his legs and into the net. The referee had no choice but to let the goal stand. Now what? After the ensuing restart at midfield, Fersina let a Dro player dribble the ball uncontested into their own goal, in a show of extreme fairness and integrity. The game ended in a 3–3 draw.

Other sports have their version of "the spirit of the game." In amateur tennis, before line judges and Hawk-Eye technology were there to call balls in and out, the unwritten rule is "when in doubt, call it in." Meaning if your opponent hits the ball and you're not sure if it caught the line or not, you show good sportsmanship by calling the ball in. Turning to cycling, and the Tour de France, if the leader in the yellow shirt has a fall or equipment failure, everyone stops until the rider is able to resume the race. That's not a rule. The racers are free to blow by the downed leader, perhaps en route to winning the single biggest bike race in the world with a purse of more than $500,000. But the integrity of the sport prevents them.

Of course, there are many examples of poor sportsmanship in soccer, basketball, and other sports, from trash talking to outright cheating. But I truly believe in the power of sports to bring out the best in humanity. It's a framework that allows us to strive to excel by doing the right thing. It's elevation through discipline and determination and adherence to a set of principles and codes.

I thought about all of this as I pondered my next move after LIU. I also went back to the teachings of Viktor Frankl around resilience and the freedom of choice. All the BS I had to deal with at LIU was behind me. I needed to shift my lens and focus on the next major decision in my life. As word got out that I was leaving LIU, I started to get approached by schools around the country, including several DI teams that had been underachieving in recent years. I had a reputation as a rebuilder, someone who could come in and turn around struggling programs.

By this point in my life, I had made the pivot into Vision Training for Life, so I brought some of that perspective to my interviews with the athletic directors. For example, I asked questions about how their programs fostered positivity in its athletes and what kind of mental health support system was in place for struggling players. I remember some of the interviewers looking at me like I had two heads, as if to say, "Listen, we just want a coach who's focused on winning; we're not looking for someone to come here and change lives." Fair enough.

I then received a call from an old friend and mentor, Bob Reasso, the legendary coach who earlier in his career had coached the likes of U.S. World Cup stars Alexi Lalas and Peter Vermes during their time at Rutgers University in New Jersey. For the past year and a half, he'd been the director of athletics at the American University in Cairo, Egypt. When he decided to come back to the States, the school asked him to find his replacement. He thought I might be interested. And I was. Though I'd traveled the world through soccer, I'd never lived abroad for an extended period of time, so the change of scenery and perspective interested me. I was just about to tell Bob "yes" when I got a call one morning from Alex Elias, my former assistant at LIU who was now the head coach at Middlebury College in Vermont.

"Hey, TJ, just wanted to let you know that there's an opening at Bard College," he said. "Bard is a different kind of place. It's special, unique. I think you'd get them and I know they'd get you."

I didn't know too much about Bard—except for the fact that they had a struggling DIII soccer program. I might be a fixer, but this one felt like a bridge too far. And yet, with my lens wide, bright, and deep, I was intrigued by the opportunity. A few days later, I had a preliminary phone interview with Bard's search committee. It was during a break in a leadership workshop I was giving at Hunter College in New York City. By the time I got back to my apartment in Brooklyn, there was a voice message from Bard saying they wanted to meet me in person. It certainly felt good to be wanted after getting pushed out at LIU.

A week later I made the trip up to the Hudson Valley of New York State. Bard put me up at an old inn in Red Hook, a town over from Annandale-on-Hudson, where the campus is located. The night before the interview, I had dinner with the senior staff from the athletic department, including the women's soccer coach and the men's basketball coach. We met at The Amsterdam, a Dutch restaurant in Rhinebeck, which felt like a sign, given my affinity for the Dutch-born Total Futbol style of play. It was clear from the get-go that they were excited to see me, and that they'd done their research.

"I love your theory of Vision Training," Bill Kelly, the women's soccer coach, said.

"Thank you, I appreciate you," I answered.

"I bought your video this morning and watched it from beginning to end."

"Wow, you didn't need to do that," I told him. "I would have brought you one."

"Not a chance," he said. "I've written several children's books myself. I know what it takes to produce something like that. It's important to support writers and artists for their work, time, and effort."

I had never heard that in my life. It immediately set a transformational, and not transactional, tone for the conversation. Then the basketball coach jumped in and asked if the same concepts of Vision Training could be applied to his sport.

"Absolutely!" I cried, suddenly feeling like I'd known these people for years. "It's all about spatial awareness and playing with your head on a swivel. Whether it's a soccer ball or a basketball, when players dribble with their heads up, they can take in the information needed to make quick, smart, well-informed decisions."

From there, the conversation picked up steam, moving into ideas of mentorship and the incredible responsibility we, as coaches and educators, have in modeling the right behavior, values, and principles.

"Good character is formed by living under conditions that demand good conduct," I said to the table. "Integrity is not innate. It's a learned behavior. Our job is to be the teacher and guide." This went on for several hours without a single dip in energy or curiosity. It was like a Talmudic study session, over craft beers and charcuterie plates. By the time my head hit the pillow back at the inn that night, I knew that I was in the right place.

That feeling intensified tenfold during my interviews the next day. I was blown away by the intentional focus on academics, in particular the process of moderation, as Bard calls it, that all students go through. During moderation, in their sophomore year, students write papers identifying their academic progress and goals and may submit a sample of work done in their program of interest. A committee of three faculty, which includes their advisor and two professors, assesses their body of work, conducts an interview, and determines whether or not to accept them into their desired course of study. It's basically an academic version of the Five Ps.

During my interview with the CFO, he told me this inspiring story about a student, Tatiana Prowell ('94), who had moderated in psychology and literature. She had planned a semester abroad at Charles University in Prague, in the Czech Republic. Under the lens-shifting moderation process, her advisor, Professor Clark Rodewald, suggested she consider a career in medicine.

"I've spent a lot of my life with doctors, and you remind me of some of the best ones," he told her. "I think you're called to do this." One of the things the two often discussed was the 1967 automobile accident that put Rodewald in a wheelchair. "We need more people in medicine that are as smart as you, but also compassionate," Rodewald said. "We don't have enough compassionate physicians."

He saw something in Prowell that she hadn't seen herself. It was a very difficult decision, but after much soul-searching and introspection, she scrapped the semester abroad and threw herself into medicine. Dr. Prowell is now a world-renowned professor of oncology at Johns Hopkins University, where she developed a life-saving modality for women with breast cancer after discovering that if they receive chemotherapy prior to surgery, their survival rate goes up significantly. In 2019, she received the John and Samuel Bard Award in Medicine and Science for her extraordinary work in the field of oncology.

That's when I was sold. I knew I wanted to be at a place that deeply cares about its students and helps empower them on their journey. It was clear to me that Bard played the game the right way by not only inspiring students to lead lives filled with integrity and purpose, but also showing them how to get there.

The Importance of Modeling High Standards

So how do we learn to play the game the right way? Because integrity is a learned behavior, the answer to that question comes down to imitation. Through imitation of others who play the game the right way, we learn to do so ourselves, and in time we pass on the behavior to those next in line. In the field of behavioral development, this process is known as modeling, and it's a key principle of Vision Training, since a wide, open lens is needed to not only recognize right from wrong, but also to act quickly and decisively in the morally correct direction.

Most of us have had an experience where we've witnessed some injustice—a disrespectful exchange between strangers, coworkers taking credit for work they didn't do, teammates taunting an opponent or flouting the rules—and not speaking up because the moment passed too quickly. Like any learned behavior, morality takes practice, especially as we get older and take on more positions of authority, whether as managers, coaches, community leaders, or parents. The way to model integrity for those around you is to practice it consciously in your own life. I learned this lesson early on in my coaching career.

As I talked about in part I of the book, one of my first coaching jobs was with the Olympic Development Program (ODP) in New Jersey in the late 1980s. My first year in the head coach role was 1987. We were coming off a very good campaign the year prior, when I was the assistant, so when the head coach left, I was handed the reins. To this day, many people consider that '87 squad to be the best N.J. U-15 ODP team of all time, with the likes of Claudio Reyna, Paul O'Donnell, Geoff Bennett, Carmelo Bagnato, and Danny Hughes.

The season started with a series of tryouts, during which my assistants and I had the unenviable task of whittling the group down from about 150 players to the final 24-man roster. It was an agonizing process due to the excess of talent in the cohort. One night after training I was unwinding at home in Lake Hopatcong, New Jersey, when the phone rang. To my surprise, it was an influential board member of the New Jersey Soccer Association, who had considerable sway within the ODP.

"Hey, TJ, how are tryouts going?" he asked.

"Extremely well," I told him. "A bit spoiled for choice with all the talent, but we're getting close to our final twenty-four. This group has the potential to do great things this year."

"That's actually what I was calling about," the board member said, his tone becoming suddenly hushed. He then proceeded to ask about a certain player who had been to the last couple of tryout sessions. I wasn't accustomed to talking about individual players, but this was a board member so I had no choice but to acquiesce.

"Sure, I know him," I said. "Nice enough kid, but not really at the level."

"That may be, but you see, he's a family friend, so I think it would be a mistake to leave him off."

I couldn't believe what I was hearing. Sure, I knew politics in New Jersey could get a little cutthroat, but I didn't think the shake-downs extended into youth soccer. The phone line went silent, with just the sound of two grown men breathing and a radio playing in the background. I knew I was in the middle of the biggest integrity test of my young career. I did my best to slow down the moment as my heart was beating excessively, taking in another deep breath of air to quiet the well of emotion that was stirring in my belly.

Of course, I knew what the right thing was to do in the moment. The player in question wasn't even close to deserving a roster spot. Meanwhile, there were at least another dozen phenomenal players who wouldn't make the cut because the talent pool was just too deep. How would it look to my players and staff if I took someone who didn't belong and sent so many deserving players packing? My credibility would have been shot, but more than that it would have sent a dead-wrong moral message to the squad. They would've come away believing that who you know is more important than how you play. I couldn't let that happen.

"I didn't accept this position so that I could be told which players to take and not take," I said firmly. "My roster is going to be filled with the twenty-four most deserving players."

"Well, that is your prerogative, TJ," the board member responded. "I'm not here to tell you what to do. I'm just warning you . . ."

His voice trailed off. We both knew how the sentence ended. Sure, a bigger person might have spoken the words, but politics has a way of stripping people of their nerve. Anyway, I'd already heard enough. I ended the call and stood in the middle of the kitchen, staring into the phone receiver for the next few minutes. Some integrity tests happen in an instant, others allow us time to think and truly consider the consequences of our actions. They're both challenging in their own way. This test was clearly the latter. It was a few days before final cuts had to be made. In that time, I continued to meet with my assistants to make sure we were focusing on the right ones. The friend of the board member didn't come up once. When we finally landed on our twenty-four-man roster for the year, his name wasn't even close.

The first day of official training, I made sure everyone on the roster knew how special they were. "This was one of the toughest decisions I've ever made as a coach," I told them during our first meeting. "We had to leave guys off who would be a lock at any other state ODP team in the country. You are here because we believe this group can achieve great things together. But it's going to require absolute commitment from every single one of you. You will all need to work harder than you've ever worked. If anyone doesn't feel like they can do that, speak up now. Because there are ten other guys who would happily take your spot."

It wasn't a threat (I never use that strategy with my teams). It was the truth. And the guys knew it and respected it. If this other player who didn't belong had been sitting in the huddle, I couldn't have given that talk with any measure of credibility. The team would have seen right through it. Instead, we entered the season with our integrity and value system in place.

And man, did we kick some tail that season. It truly was the most elite squad of U-15s that I had ever witnessed, let alone coached. We absolutely annihilated teams, even the better ones who should have given us a match. At the end of the campaign, every one of our starting eleven made the regional camp, something that had never happened before.

I wish I could tell you the story had a happy ending, maybe with a call from the board member congratulating the squad on all its success. In fact, I never heard from the individual again. When the next season rolled around, I was simply dropped from the program. No phone call or explanation was ever given. A new coach was brought on. And guess what? The player in question made the team.

It would have been easy to turn sour grapes over the situation. But when I think back on the experience, I know it put me at a moral crossroads, and that I chose the right path. Moreover, my players knew it too. The political machinations at ODP weren't a secret. The parents all understood what was going on, which means the boys were aware on some level too. Taking a 360-degree view of the situation, and also considering the short- and long-term consequences of my actions, I was able to model the right behavior for my team and sleep comfortably at night knowing I did the right thing. The impact of that decision, as twenty-four young men turned into adults with lives of their own, can never be known. This is the beauty of it: when we do the right thing, we never know how far the influence will travel or how many lives it will touch.

The Speed of Ethical Thinking

Now I want to shift gears and talk about fast-moving integrity tests. These are the moments I alluded to earlier that happen so quickly that it's all too easy to not do the right thing, simply because you didn't have time to act. How do we prepare for this? Through rigorous adherence to the Five Ps. Perceive what's happening around you, constantly process the information, use early diligent planning to know how you want to respond in certain challenging situations, perform well in these moments, and persist by committing to doing the right thing over and over. You'll make mistakes since you're not perfect, but by applying the Five Ps we can all establish a personal code of ethics based on integrity and moral values.

One of my favorite examples of this involves Landon Donovan, among the greatest U.S. Men's National Team players of all time; he had the most assists as an international player and is tied for the most goals with his former teammate Clint Dempsey. As impressive as Donovan's playing stats are, his off-the-field achievements are just as noteworthy in my book. For example, he's always been very open about his battles with depression and is an advocate for improved mental health support in professional sports.

I never coached Donovan, but I had the chance to meet him at the United Soccer Coaches Convention in California back in 2018. He was in the process of transitioning from a player to a coach and would soon be named the inaugural manager of the San Diego Loyal, a team in the USL Championship that he had helped found.

"I really like what you're doing with the Vision Training," Donovan said, as we chatted amicably at the Anaheim Convention Center after he received the Walt Chyzowych Distinguished Playing Career Award. "How can I learn more about it for myself?" Here I was meeting the most decorated player in the history of U.S. Men's Soccer and he's the one handing out compliments. I knew instantly that he was a class act.

"That's kind of you, Landon," I said. "I'd be happy to send you more materials as you settle into the coaching life."

We talked for a few more minutes before parting ways for our next appointment at the conference. It's always nice when a person you've admired and respected from afar turns out to be a warm and approachable person up close. And that was very much the impression I had of Donovan after that first meeting. I sent him the Vision Training materials, as promised, but didn't think too much about him again until about a year later, when he made international headlines over an incident involving his newly formed Loyal.

Here's the moment of fast-acting moral rectitude that I wanted to share. As the story goes, the Loyal were in the final minutes of the first half of a match against the Phoenix Rising, leading by a score of 3–1, when a Rising player used a homophobic slur against one of San Diego's midfielders. During the halftime break, Donovan gathered his team in the locker room with a difficult decision to make. He could pay lip service to the incident and move on to second half strategies. He could use it as a rallying cry to motivate his squad to thrash the Rising even harder in the final forty-five. Or he could take the opportunity to make a meaningful stand against unacceptable, discriminatory behavior.

Moments later, the Loyal emerged from the tunnel and seemed ready to take the field. Instead, every single player took a knee on the sideline, a show of solidarity for their slandered teammate and a defiant protest against bigotry. Donovan did the right thing, acting clearly and decisively when it would have been so easy to look the other way. In fact, the coach of the Rising, in disbelief over Donovan's decision, actually tried to argue that slurs and name-calling were just "trash talk and a part of soccer."

What motivated Donovan to see right from wrong so clearly? As details of the incident emerged in the media, I was struck by how the Five Ps were part of the answer to this question. I can't say whether he had read the materials on Vision Training that I had sent him and was actively implementing the Five Ps. Nevertheless, it's a shining example of the principles I preach.

The whole story actually began a week earlier, at another match against the Los Angeles Galaxy in which a different Loyal player was also the target of bigotry, this time racial. In that instance, Donovan admitted that he and his squad did not act decisively enough.

"We should have done something in the moment when [our player] was racially abused," he said in a video statement posted on the Loyal's Twitter feed. "That was our regret, from our players, from me, I wish we would have done something."

And yet, from my perspective, Donovan *had* done something. Through his application of the first P, perceive, he had witnessed the situation and took in as much information as possible, which he then processed, applying the second P. Seeing how hurtful the incident had been, he and his club then formulated a plan, the third P, which amounted to a full commitment to taking a stand against all future acts of racism, homophobia, and bigotry. "So much so that on our sign boards, we made a statement saying, 'I will act, I will speak,'" Donovan explained. "If something happens, I'm going to speak about it, I'm going to act about it."

One week later, the Loyal had the chance to stand behind their words. Donovan admitted that the halftime intermission made for an incredibly difficult twenty minutes, not least of which because of the serious beating they were putting on Phoenix. "That's a great feeling as a soccer player," Donovan said, explaining that in the passion of the moment, many of the guys wanted to keep playing. "But, if we wanted to be true to who we are as a club, we had to speak and we had to act." The Loyal would have been willing to play the second half if the Rising player who made the slur was taken out, either by the referee or by Phoenix's coach. The ref said he couldn't make the call because he hadn't heard the slur. Phoenix's coach flat-out refused to sub the player out.

"Our guys, to their immense credit, said 'we're not going to stand for this,'" Donovan continued. "It was very clear in that moment that we were giving up all hopes of making the playoffs [by forfeiting the match], even as we were beating one of the best teams in the league handily, but the guys said it doesn't matter. There are more important things in life and we have to stick up for what we believe in. I have tremendous pride in this group and I'm really proud of this organization that I get to be a part of."

Throughout his career, Landon Donovan always played the game the right way. The fact that he set up as many goals as he scored—through a combination of vision and selflessness—is a testament to that. As a manager, he worked hard to establish a club culture based on a clear set of moral values, which he vigilantly and rigorously upholds. The incident with the Phoenix Rising was the club's biggest test, and under Donovan's clear-eyed leadership, they passed it with flying colors. The players were right—taking the forfeit kept the Loyal out of the 2020 playoffs. But guess what? They made it the following year, and the year after too. Playing the game the right way isn't just the moral choice. It's often the winning one too. You'll never regret taking the path of integrity. But you will regret not standing up for someone.

In the middle of writing this book, I discussed this topic while visiting my cousin George Hayduchok and his wife, Nadine, at their home in Ithaca, New York. George is a graduate of Cornell, with degrees in engineering and law. Full transparency, he's also one of my heroes. Although he's a bit younger, I've always admired his approach to life, which is the same one he brings to his career as the owner of a software development and services company called Mavro Imaging.

Every one of George's employees and hundreds of customers is treated fairly and generously. George's deep gratitude for his team and customers has created a culture of loyalty and success, as evidenced by two key statistics: Mavro's historical employee retention rate stands at 97 percent and the company has never lost a customer to a competing vendor. That is unheard of in today's business world.

While George's generosity is legendary, the real reason for Mavro's success, I'd argue, is the integrity that he brings to every business decision. When I pressed him on this process, he shared these words: "You have to have a plan and think about integrity in advance. You have to be armed with it. It doesn't just happen on its own. If you have to debate the decision in your head without an established framework, it's too late. Your mindset must already be there. I go into each and every day with integrity as a priority. Therefore, when confronted with an ethical dilemma, primed with integrity, the decision is an easy one as I already know what to do. There's no debate. It is essential that I walk the talk since my choices, actions, and behavior directly impact every employee in my company and each of my customers."

This is another example of the Five Ps in motion. George's wide, open lens enables him to take in the whole of his company, down to the individual employee and customer, and make decisions that will serve both camps equally well. In George's latest end-of-the-year newsletter, he pledged the following: "Mavro will continue to place our most valuable assets first—treating customers as friends and team members as family."

Throughout my life, I've been fortunate to have influences like my cousin George, people with a strong moral compass who have helped me appreciate the value of playing the game the right way. Of course, each of us is guided by our own code of conduct, so we are not dealing in absolute rights and wrongs here. The key is to move through life with intention, awareness, and reflection so that you're in a constant state of self-improvement. This is how the best players keep getting better. By constantly scanning the field, they're able to recognize the greatness in others and incorporate it into their own game. The same process happens in life. Look for the positive examples and follow them. Then become the example for others to follow. This takes me to the next big lesson of Vision Training: the importance of making everyone around you better.

Chapter Eight

MAKE EVERYONE AROUND YOU BETTER

Having spent the better part of four decades on college campuses, I've heard plenty of debate around moral obligation, usually by people who are a lot more learned than me. I can't tell you if Kant or Kierkegaard had it right, or where the line is between moral and legal responsibility. I can only tell you what I believe, which is that if you have the opportunity to make the world a better place, go ahead and do it.

I think most people would probably go along with that. The trick is finding those opportunities, day in and day out. By keeping your lens wide, bright, and deep, you'll be able to pick up on moments for good that otherwise might have passed you by. It goes back to the first of the Five Ps: perception, or the spark that opens up your eyes to the world around you. Sometimes the moments are big, maybe noticing that a friend or loved one is hurting based on something in their body language or demeanor. Other moments are small and mundane and, as a result, easy to ignore, like the bit of trash on the street that gets stepped over by thousands of people until one of them decides to pick it up. That reminds me of a story, one that sheds light on the link between perception and selflessness.

As a proud Ukrainian, I relish an opportunity to get back to the homeland. My first Vision Training trip coincided with the Maidan protests during Russia's invasion and annexation of Crimea in 2013. At that time, I trained the coaches and youth players from Zirka FC in Kiev. Five years later, I got the chance to return when a close friend in Brooklyn connected me with a Ukrainian philanthropist who supported the local football club in Berezhany, a small city in the northwest corner of the country, a couple hours' drive from Lviv. This time, I invited my business partner, Len. Because we were both Ukrainian, I could see it being an incredibly moving experience for the two of us.

Len and I landed in Lviv airport and made the sixty-mile journey to Berezhany. It was extremely slow-going because the road was strewn with crater-size potholes, an indelible image of the impoverished nation, but eventually we reached the outskirts of the city, which is more of an old-world village, with a population of just under ten thousand. As we entered the city center, the road switched from dirt to pavement for a quarter-mile stretch.

We were greeted at the one hotel in town by Stepan, the president of the soccer club. After exchanging a few short pleasantries, I asked him why only one section of road was paved.

"That's all we had money for," he answered matter-of-factly. I'd been in impoverished places before, but this was a whole new level. One nice strip of paved asphalt and shops and everything else dirt, rubble, and potholes big enough to lose a car in.

Len and I checked into the hotel, rested up for an hour or so, and then made our way to the local high school, where we'd be leading a Vision Training session for coaches from the area, before our main session with the senior team that evening. About thirty minutes in, I was desperate for the bathroom—my constitution was still adjusting to the local cuisine.

"Down in the basement," one of the coaches shouted, gesturing to a small doorway at the far end of the gym. I made a beeline for the exit and snaked my way down into the depths of the building. If the road conditions around Berezhany had been rough, they were nothing compared to the school bathroom. The only light came from a small, grime-covered window, the walls were wet with condensation, and instead of toilet stalls, there were a few holes in the ground separated by wobbly dividers. It was bleak.

I'll spare you any more details. Suffice to say, the experience made me appreciate how little the people of Berezhany had, and of course how fortunate I was with all my first-world comforts back home. I returned to the gym and finished the clinic with Len. The coaches were incredibly receptive and appreciative, so we left on a high note.

"Let's walk to the stadium for the next session," Stepan said as we exited the high school. It was a beautiful night in Berezhany. As we strolled past the river that winds its way through the village, chatting amicably about soccer, Len suddenly veered off from the group. When he bent over, I thought maybe his shoelace had come untied. But no, he was simply picking up empty bags of potato chips and other debris that was littering the sidewalk. I smiled knowingly.

As I explained earlier in the book, Len was my Yoda when it came to learning the fundamentals of Vision Training soccer. We've evolved the program together over the years, but I credit him with many of the original concepts. The life training piece that's come out of it is more mine (I don't say *all* mine because so many people have influenced my thinking over time). That meant a switching of roles for Len and me when it comes to lessons like the Five Ps, the Three Ls, and making the world a better place.

Picking up litter was one of my earliest teachings. It's something I've done as a matter of course for most of my adult life. Whether I'm walking through the woods of upstate New York or the streets of downtown Brooklyn, if I see a piece of errant trash, I always pick it up and toss it in the nearest garbage can. As you might expect, it's a more demanding ritual in the city. One time I was walking to LIU when I came across an entire trash can that had been knocked over into the city street. I put down my gym bag on the sidewalk and started to toss the loose trash into the metal can. It was rush hour, so cars were whizzing by and pedestrians were bumping into me. I finally got the last of the litter into the bin and hoisted it upright back onto the sidewalk. Just then I heard a car horn give a few light honks. I looked up and the woman in the driver's seat was giving me a huge smile and her two teenage passengers in the back seat were giving me a huge thumbs-up.

That experience, which couldn't have taken more than a minute or two, had me glowing all day long. Here it is nearly ten years later, and it still makes me smile. That's the magic of selfless living. And there's no shortage of research showing how doing good by others makes you feel better yourself, and might even help you live longer. Consider the 2015 study conducted by researchers at the University of California San Diego's School of Medicine, which found that people who are more giving and grateful maintain better heart health, less inflammation, and healthier heart rhythms. The study also found that acts of altruism are effective at warding off depression, stress, and anxiety, all of which can add to the risk of heart disease.

Other studies have found that selflessness can improve intimacy in relationships through the release of oxytocin, a neuropeptide that's known to stimulate prosocial behaviors, such as trust, generosity, and affection. Giving improves psychological health and mental strength by reducing toxic emotions, such as jealousy, frustration, and regret. It can even help you get a better night's sleep by quieting your mind and relaxing your body before bedtime.

Okay, back to Berezhany and my early evening stroll to the stadium. Watching Len pick up that piece of trash was as gratifying as seeing one of my players on the pitch check his shoulder five times in ten seconds. It was the ripple effect in action, or as I like to say, the way one good deed begets another. Selflessness is truly contagious.

Standing on the riverbank, I had another flashback to Brooklyn, this one to my first apartment there, a fourth-floor walk-up on Smith Street in Carroll Gardens. As was customary in that kind of building, delivery people would leave packages in the small lobby just inside the main entrance. I didn't know anyone in the building, but I knew most of their names, which were displayed on the inside mailbox, so anytime I came home to a package on the floor, I picked it up and left it outside the recipient's apartment door. This went on for a few weeks—a package for 4B one day, 2A the next, 3D the day after that, and so on.

I often tell this story in my Vision Training for Life workshops, and whenever I do, I pause at this point and ask the audience why they think I did this. "Because you're a nice guy," some people answer. "So nobody trips over the packages," others will say. Both are true. But the answer I give is much simpler.

"Because I could," I tell them. "I have two open arms and it's easy for me to pick up a package and leave it for someone who might be loaded down with groceries or juggling a couple toddlers when they reach home. This was something I could do, so I did it."

Fast-forward a few months. I returned home from a recruiting trip and walked up the stairs to find a package outside my front door. "That's really nice," I thought to myself. Maybe a week later, I reached the building, passed through the main entrance, and saw a dad with a baby in his arms and a four-year-old girl at his feet, about to climb the first flight of stairs.

"Daddy, wait," the girl said suddenly, tugging on his arm and pulling him back toward the lobby. "I want to get a package to give to someone in the building today."

It was such a wow moment. Here was this four-year-old girl who learned that giving is a good thing. That was never my intent. I didn't deliver packages with the hope of influencing this young child. But that was the consequence. We all have opportunities every single day to do small acts of kindness and we don't know how far or how deep the impact will be.

As Len, Stepan, and I got closer to the stadium, the pathway became busier with people out enjoying the pleasant evening. A couple minutes after Len retrieved the trash, I spotted a flattened soda can on the ground. It had obviously been there for some time. I bent down and picked it up. Len and I traded smiles. Stepan, meanwhile, looked at us like we were nuts.

This went on for the remainder of the walk to the stadium, Len and I casually collecting trash and depositing it in the garbage cans that were stationed along the way. We then went about our business, leading a group of talented Ukrainian players through the principles of Vision Training. It's always a huge rush to hear myself and Len explain the concepts of the program in our mother tongue, even if some of it's a bit rusty at times. The response from the players was incredible, such that by the end of the session their awareness and decision-making had clearly improved.

"Amazing," Stepan said to us after the session.

"They're a coachable lot," I answered. "That made our job a lot easier."

It was pushing nine o'clock at this point and Len and I had been traveling for the past twenty-four hours. I couldn't wait to get back to the hotel, but I had a feeling that wasn't in the cards just yet.

"Come, let's eat," Stepan said, confirming my hunch.

We ended up at a classic Ukrainian restaurant, a crowded, dimly lit spot that served big bowls of borscht and varenyky (or pierogies) of every flavor. And, of course, vodka. Shot after shot of vodka, to the point where Len and I had to start pretending to drink.

Naturally, as the vodka flowed, so did the conversation. Stepan was full of hope for the coming season, talking excitedly about the talent and depth in the senior squad. Then, suddenly, he grew quiet. I could see that his lens had shifted.

"I've been thinking," he started. "The impact of Vision Training has been incredible. It's helped elevate the senior team to the next level. But it's our youth clubs which could really benefit. What if we were to plant the seeds in them and watch them sprout and spread, not just on the football field, but throughout the entire community? Wouldn't that have more of an impact?"

Len and I stared blankly for a moment. Stepan certainly was a good person, but his focus had always been on making his football club better. In his mind, it was the one area of control in a sea of chaos. Yet here he was imagining the possibility of making his community a better place. It was a remarkable transformation.

"Stepan, I think you're absolutely right," I answered finally. "And we'd love to help."

The evening ended soon after that exchange. We stumbled out of the restaurant, our bellies full, and headed back to the hotel, with Stepan leading the way. Just then, a breeze kicked up a sheet of newspaper that had been lying on the sidewalk. Like a cat, Stepan sprung and grabbed it in midair.

"Aha!" he cried triumphantly, then crumpled up the paper and dropped it into the nearest trash bin.

The Ripple Effect in Overdrive

One of the most powerful examples of the ripple effect from my life started at the 2019 United Soccer Coaches Convention in Chicago. The largest annual gathering of soccer coaches nationwide, the event draws tens of thousands of attendees from all over the country and world for a week of seminars, panel talks, exhibitions, and more. I was there to lead a session titled "How to Get Your Players to Make the Best Decisions." The year prior, our event had been standing room only with an audience of over a thousand. But this year we were given the Saturday morning slot. I forgot how most of the coaches like to party long and hard into the night on Friday. Not only that, it was an absolutely frigid January morning in the Windy City.

I remember feeling a little deflated as I walked onto the stage that had been set up in the convention center and saw a crowd of maybe fifty coaches on hand. But it ended up being a good lesson in the importance of quality over quantity, because all fifty were locked in throughout the entire session. They were serious about their craft and I was grateful that they believed enough in what I had to teach them to make it out of bed early on a Saturday.

That was my state of mind when a woman approached me after the session. She had a trim, athletic build, like most people at the conference, and an even healthier smile.

"Hi, my name is Karen Wright," she said warmly, reaching out her hand.

"Hi, Karen, I'm TJ," I said. "Thank you for coming out on a cold winter morning."

"Thank *you*," she replied. "I run a small youth soccer club in Carlton, Oregon, and boy, could our kids benefit from your knowledge and what you have to say."

"We have Vision Training videos for sale," I started to say, but Karen kept going.

"We're a nonprofit, so there's nothing in the budget to pay you. But if we could just get you out to Oregon for a few days, I think you'd be amazed by our kids. Like I said, they could really use some wisdom from a coach like you."

I'm not a very good businessman, but even I know I couldn't afford to fly across the country to run a free camp in rural Oregon for a couple dozen youth players. Yet my lens was open wide and there was something in Karen's demeanor that made me think this was something I needed to consider. I felt deeply attuned to her goodness and generosity of spirit.

"Did I mention we also have a winery, Ken Wright Cellars?" Karen added with a smile. "You can stay in the loft for free and drink the best pinot noir in the country."

"Sold," I said. With that, a fresh pebble had been dropped. I couldn't wait to see how far its ripples would extend.

Six months later I was on a flight from New York to Portland to run a summer clinic at the Yamhill Carlton Soccer Club. Since my first meeting in Chicago with Karen, I'd learned a bit more about the organization, which Karen had started on a shoestring budget in 2013. One of the most serious issues facing soccer in the U.S. is the "pay to play" model of the sport at the youth level. It's not unusual for clubs to charge $2,000 to $3,000 a year in registration fees, not counting all the added costs, from uniforms to travel. That keeps hundreds of thousands of families out of the game, especially in poor parts of the country, like rural Oregon. Karen recognized the inherent unfairness in this system and decided to do something about it. I couldn't wait to learn more.

She was kind enough to pick me up at the airport. As we got onto the highway, we passed by various homeless encampments on the side of the road. Karen vented her frustration with the local government for failing to provide better resources for the underserved. I certainly understood her frustration, though in that moment I was simply grateful for this opportunity to be in Oregon with her having what I knew would be an enormously positive experience. I said as much from the passenger seat.

"Thank you for that, TJ," she replied. "I get a little fired up over this stuff sometimes. I'm grateful to have you here. Wait until you see the place."

As we pulled up to the club, a group of about ten kids of varying ages were engaged in a spirited game of pickup on a turf pitch. We sat watching from the car for a few minutes.

"I like seeing the mixed ages out there," I said.

"That's been the model from the beginning," Karen explained. "It's a way for all the kids of the community to get to know each other and look after one another. When a new player joins the club, we tell them that they need to look out for anyone who is younger than them, smaller than them, or less skilled at soccer than them. It creates a sense of mentorship that extends out into the community as a whole."

We got out of the car and made our way toward the field. I noticed a dumpster that was filled to the brim with glass bottles and aluminum cans.

"We'll take that down to the redemption center this week," Karen said. "There are others just like it all over town. It should be a pretty good haul."

This was the year-round deposit return bottle-and-can drive that Karen had mentioned in one of our follow-up planning calls after our first meeting in Chicago. Every year, the club received hundreds of thousands of recyclables from local residents and used the proceeds to fund the Yamhill Carlton Soccer Club Scholarship Program. Whereas most scholarships are reserved for a select few, this one was extended to every single member of the club. They call it a scholarship but really it's a way to ensure that any kid in Carlton County who wants to play soccer can do so for free. Actually, that's not true. There is an annual registration fee. Care to guess how much? Fifteen dollars! That wouldn't even get you thirty minutes of training at most clubs around the country.

Karen and her club are a remarkable example of how a wide, open lens can reveal opportunities for change. What struck me even more during my five-day stint in Oregon was how the positive vibes established at the club extend out into the community. No one embodied this more than a twelve-year-old young man named Lucas Partin who was among the scrum of mixed-age players engaged in pickup when I arrived that first day. As Karen and I stood there watching the game, there were several moments when Lucas showed some act of kindness to a younger player—slowing the game down so that a slower player could catch up, selflessly passing the ball instead of scoring an easy tap-in, joyously lifting a much smaller kid onto his shoulders after the youngster cleanly kicked the ball.

"That's a special kid there," Karen said.

"I can see that," I said admiringly. "What's his story?"

"Lucas has been with us from the beginning," she answered. "He's a shining example of what can happen when kids are given the chance to be leaders in the community. Lucas loves to work with younger kids in the program. It started with him hanging around after his own practice to help the coaches with the younger classes. Then he became an official volunteer coach. He gets true pleasure in seeing other people be successful. He knows exactly how much pressure to put on a child in training to allow them to succeed. Last year he put in more than three hundred volunteer hours. Now all the kids want to be like him. The third graders want to help the first graders. The first graders want to help the preschoolers. It's been incredible watching it catch on."

Later that afternoon, I had the chance to work with Lucas in person when he showed up for my Vision Training coach's seminar. Karen had asked if he could sit in on the session. "He's a little young," I thought to myself, but then remembered how well he interacted with the younger players on the training pitch. Sure enough, Lucas more than held his own in the course, both in the classroom portion and the on-field instructional. To this day, he's the youngest person to become a certified Vision Training soccer coach.

The next day, Lucas assisted me during multiple Vision Training sessions with kids of all ages from the club. He's a quick study, as you might expect, so within a single coach's session, he'd been able to absorb the language of Vision Training and was now communicating it to the kids, teaching them the importance of playing "eyes up" ball and taking constant peeks to know where they were on the field relative to other players and not to shout for the ball.

I ran three more sessions over the course of my stay in Oregon. The response from the community was so positive that I also offered a Vision Training for Life workshop on the last night of my stay. We ended up doing it in the tasting room of Karen and Ken's winery. I was used to running my workshops in big cities for singular groups, whether athletic directors or government officials. But this was rural Oregon, so we ended up with a far more eclectic group. The superintendent of schools made it out, as did a local astronomer of some renown. A single mom showed up with her twelve- and sixteen-year-old sons. Another mom brought her fourteen-year-old daughter. And, of course, Lucas was there, along with his mom, Michelle, eager to soak in whatever new information he could.

I opened the workshop as I normally do, by getting the group to brainstorm the various qualities that are shared by all transformational leaders. After a few seconds, a fourteen-year-old girl raised her hand.

"Please share," I said.

"Compassion," she answered. "Transformative leaders must be compassionate."

"Wow," I thought to myself. "This is going to be damn good." And it was. In the opening brainstorm alone, we came up with thirty-seven qualities of transformational leadership—curious, communicative, risk-tolerant, inspirational, charismatic, adaptable, to name a few. To this day, it was the best workshop I've ever led and I believe a big reason for that was the shared value system that the community had established through Karen's soccer club. The ripple effect of what Karen started five years earlier had permeated every corner of the Yamhill-Carlton community. Then it made its way to

Chicago, where on a frigid January morning, it touched me. Because my own lens was wide, bright, and deep, I was able to see that Karen was up to something very special, and so now I'm part of the ripple. In fact, I've been back to the club every year since, and Yamhill Carlton Soccer Club is now the first fully accredited Vision Training program in all of Oregon.

Before my most recent visit there, I hopped on a planning call with Karen. I always like to open catch-up calls by sharing highlights or moments of gratitude from our respective lives. It's so easy to jump right into the business at hand and ignore the opportunity for human connection.

"So what's new in Carlton?" I asked Karen.

"It's been a wonderful week," she replied. "We had our first toddler/pre-K free time this week and got them started on Vision Training with a game of puppies in the park, which is just our version of sharks and minnows. It applies all your principles—hiding the ball, picking their heads up to find the free space in the park, spinning away from the dog catcher."

"The fact that you're able to introduce these concepts to three- and four-year-olds is absolutely wonderful," I said. "It fills my heart with joy, truly."

"Oh, then you're going to love this," Karen added. "Yesterday I was walking through town with a bunch of fourth-grade girls. Alexis and Makenna—you remember them?"

"Of course I do," I said.

"As we crossed the street, they were using Vision Training principles, taking peeks over their shoulders to check that the group was intact. Nobody told them to do this. They were instinctively looking out for one another to make sure everyone was safe."

The image of those fourth-graders crossing the street in

downtown Carlton is everything Vision Training can be. Through the experience of consistently playing eyes-up soccer, they had learned to see the field with a wide, open lens. Now they could apply that same perspective to life and use it to make the world a better, safer place.

Gleaning Ways to Give Back

In the spring of 2021, I experienced another ripple effect of my own at Bard. It began, like so many positive experiences in my life, with a moment of synchronicity. I liked to treat myself to a meal out on Friday nights. I was still getting to know the good people from my community, so I often took these meals alone, which I've never had a problem with, since it usually resulted in some new encounter.

I was getting ready to leave my apartment on Broadway, the main road through the village of Tivoli. The weather in upstate New York was starting to turn, so there was a chill in the air. I began to grab my Bard soccer sweatshirt, but then reached instead for the one emblazoned in red with the letters BPI, short for Bard Prison Initiative. Several months earlier I had attended a screening of *College Behind Bars*, a fascinating PBS documentary directed by Lynn Novick, which chronicles the story of a dozen incarcerated men and women who received top-tier college degrees from within the correctional system. I was so inspired by this example of the transformative power of education that I pledged a small gift of financial support for BPI immediately after the screening. The sweatshirt was a thank-you gift from the organization.

I made my way out of the apartment and walked about one hundred yards to GioBatta, a wonderful Italian restaurant owned by my friends Francesco and Michelle Buitoni, in the village of Tivoli. As I climbed the short flight of wooden steps leading to the entrance, I noticed a couple of men seated in the window. One was Dr. Leon Botstein, the president of Bard College. The other was Max Kenner, the Bard alumni and founder of BPI. He was looking at me through the glass with a big smile. I pointed down at my sweatshirt and we both gave a big thumbs-up.

As I entered GioBatta, Max gestured for me to come over. I didn't want to impose on their meal, but I figured a quick hello couldn't hurt. Plus it was an opportunity to let Max know how much I appreciated his work.

"Love the sweatshirt," Max said.

"It's become my favorite," I answered. "I don't want to interrupt your dinner, but I wanted to say how grateful I am for the work that you do. I talk about it all the time."

"What do you mean?" Max asked.

"I just took over the men's soccer program at Bard," I explained. "But I also do workshops on transformative leadership, including finding ways of giving back and being more selfless. I always include your story, because it is such a powerful example of how having an open lens and seeing things from a different perspective can be the spark for incredible change."

As the story goes, Max was an undergraduate at Bard in 1998 when, as part of his studies of social justice, he made the uncomfortable discovery that of the 72,000 men and women in the New York State prison system, roughly 80 percent were from New York City, where at the time only about half of all high school students made it to graduation. That realization was the spark that started him on a mission to find new and better ways to help the incarcerated cast their lives in a new light through the power of learning and higher education. The result was the Bard Prison Initiative, which, in Max's own words, "is a very simple experiment: What happens when we provide the kind of education that traditionally in the U.S. is only provided to lucky, privileged, rich people to others?"

If you haven't seen the documentary yet, I encourage you to do so, because it answers the question in the most positive and inspiring way. It's eye-opening to see inmates from maximum-security prisons in upstate New York using the same curriculum as Bard students and maintaining the same standard of academic rigor and commitment. In one of the documentary's most memorable scenes, the BPIU debate team goes up against Harvard over the issue of whether public schools in the United States should have the ability to deny enrollment to undocumented students. BPI's well-deserved victory over its Ivy League adversary made national headlines, completely changing the narrative about who people in prison are and what they're capable of, given the opportunity and resources.

The entire four-part series gave me chills, but the scene that spoke to me the most came during the commencement scene in the last episode. Shawnta Montgomery, since released from prison, is among the graduates on hand. As we watch her receive her diploma from Bard president Leon Botstein, she makes this observation: "BPI has given me a new pair of eyes to recognize certain cycles in life and see how I don't want to be a part of certain things anymore." She goes on to talk about the humanizing effect of the program and how the graduation ceremony felt like a utopia.

BPI is as powerful an example as I know of how the shifting of one's lens can have life-changing effects. And the fact is clearly born out in the data. BPI participants have a recidivism rate of less than 4 percent, compared to the national average of 43 percent. According to a study from RAND, for every dollar that's invested in the program, the country saves five dollars in re-incarceration costs over three years.

Since Max Kenner first had the spark as a student at Bard in the late 1990s, BPI has expanded to seven prisons in New York State and conferred more than six hundred degrees to prisoners at these campuses. The mission has even gone global, with partnerships across the Americas, Africa, and Europe. BPI is a study in perception, the first P, but also persistence, the last P. As Max put it in a 2021 interview, "Fifteen years ago, if you worked in this space, you would get up in the morning, put your suit on and get ready for people to hate you because of what you did for a living. That dynamic has been completely reversed. I don't think that reversal has happened in the last 12 months. That reversal has happened gradually over the last 20 years."

A few weeks after our encounter at the Italian restaurant, Max Kenner was very much on my mind as I took my morning walk through the Hudson Valley countryside. Autumn was in full swing in upstate New York, with a thin layer of frost on the ground, so I might have even had my favorite BPI sweatshirt on. At one point, my regular walking route took me through Greig Farm, a family-owned, pick-your-own establishment located about ten minutes from Bard's campus. The farm was started in the 1940s by Marion and Robert Greig and is now run by their son Norman, who along with his team has made it a centerpiece of the local community, for example by welcoming artists and entrepreneurs to open their businesses on the farm. The public walking trails that skirt the perimeter of the three-hundred-plus-acre property—filled with apple orchards, asparagus, pumpkin patches, strawberry fields, and more—are another example of Greig Farm's communal spirit. As you might imagine, it's my kind of place.

The only nagging thought I had that morning as I passed through the farm was the overabundance of unpicked apples, some of which had already fallen to the ground. It made me sad, especially given how many hungry mouths could really benefit from the nourishment; the child poverty rate in some parts of New York is above 50 percent, or three times the national average. "This is no good," I thought to myself, surveying the thousands of apples around me that would soon turn into worm food.

I thought about Max Kenner and how his perception of the link between education and crime led to a hugely impactful prison reform movement. Just then I was approached on the trail by a young couple out walking with their dog.

"Beautiful day," I said.

"It sure is," the woman answered. "The foliage is something else this year. And look at the fruit on the trees. Some of those apples are about ready to burst."

"I was just thinking about that," I responded. "It's a shame so many of them go to waste."

"It really is," the man said, joining the conversation. "But we just can't get enough people in to pick them."

"Do you work here?" I asked.

"I do," he answered, then stuck out his hand to shake. "Rob Greig. My dad, Norman, owns the farm."

Synchronicity had struck again. As I talked about earlier in the book, it's important to recognize chance opportunities and make the most of them. Standing by an orchard field on a glorious fall day, I knew that I was experiencing just such a moment and that I needed to act quickly.

"TJ Kostecky," I said. "I'm the new head soccer coach at Bard. You know, I've got plenty of students at the college who could help."

"Shoot me an email," Rob said.

"I will do that," I promised. We chatted for a few more minutes, then went on our way. I was buzzing the whole way home, processing the encounter and imagining the possibilities.

As it turned out, there was more synchronicity in store for me that day. My "Weird Coincidence Scale," if you remember that from chapter six, must have been off the charts. After my morning walk, I had gone about the business of the day. Evening came and I made my way down to Santa Fe, a great Mexican spot in downtown Tivoli. The place was hopping, but I managed to grab the last open seat at the bar. I settled down, ordered a drink, and introduced myself to the person sitting next to me, as was customary in the village.

"How you doing, TJ?" the man said. "My name is Norman Greig."

That was the beginning of a voluntary initiative that would come to be known as Low Hanging Fruit. That night at the bar, I told Norman about my run-in with Rob on the trail and the nascent idea to bring in Bard students to help pick leftover apples (or "glean," to use the technical term) and distribute them to shelters and food centers in the area.

"Let's do it," was his unequivocal response. He was eager to engage more with the college—for example, sharing more about their sustainable farming practices with students enrolled in the environmental sciences.

We had missed the window on this harvest, so we set our sights on the following autumn. That left plenty of time to plan, the third P. One of my first calls was to a former player of mine named Jack Loud, who decided to stop playing soccer after his sophomore year so that he could focus more on sustainability, which had become his main passion.

"Jack, I've been walking Greig Farm and they have all these left-over apples that are going to waste. What do you think, can we help?"

"Definitely," he said. "I'm president of the Sustainability Club now. Let me drive this project. We can totally get it done."

"You're on," I said. It had been hard losing Jack as a player, but it was now abundantly clear that by maintaining a wide, open, bright lens, he was on the right path.

Jack connected me with Laurie Husted, who runs the Office of Sustainability at Bard. We had three meetings fall through (the project was on top of everyone's already full plates) but through sheer persistence the three of us eventually connected. That's when things really started to snowball. We worked through the many logistics. How many gleaning sessions could we take on? Just apples, or other fruits? Who would deliver the fruit? Who would receive it? It was a ton of work, but everyone involved was coming from a place of passion, so it never felt onerous. We were finding deeper meaning and forming deeper connections.

Winter turned to spring, spring to summer, and eventually it was harvest time again. We settled on a date in September for the first gleaning session, which would mainly consist of Bard athletes; students from other parts of the college would step up for later sessions. That morning, members of the women's and men's soccer teams, and the track and cross-country squads, along with other passionate students from Bard, filled a couple of vans on campus and made their way to the farm.

Norman met us at the entrance and took us to the farthest corner of the orchard, where apples almost never get picked. He showed us the proper way to glean an apple—cupping it in your hand, raising it above the branch, and gently twisting, so as not to damage the fruiting spurs for next year's harvest.

At that point, the students scattered about the orchard in small groups, each with an apple box in hand that would soon be brimming with the most beautiful array of apples, including Gala, McIntosh, and Macouns.

"Coach, Coach, come check this out," one of the students cried. It was CeDaniel Sumpter from the track team. I ran over to see his discovery. In the palm of his hand sat a bright red Mcintosh apple with a small, exquisite yellow heart on it. It was a powerful image and a perfect affirmation of the work we were doing. A week later I received a text from CeDaniel. He explained that he had never gleaned before, and only days earlier he had discussed the topic with a close friend. The following day, he learned about the Low Hanging Fruit project. Synchronicity had intervened once again. "The surreal experience of speaking about something and then coincidentally being able to do it shortly after is something to not overlook as well," he wrote. "The entire experience was one of connection and vibrational happenstance."

Other students wrote to me after the apple gleaning. I love this message from Cole Ewalt, a student from Hawaii on our men's soccer team: "One thing that stood out to me was the manner in which everyone at the farm went about their work," he wrote. "Starting with gratitude and appreciation for the property and opportunity, we then moved into the actual service project, gleaning apples for a food shelter in Red Hook. As I took on each individual apple, making sure to gently twist and separate from the branch, so as not to bruise the outside, I noticed how happy everyone was in the simple act of service. I was surprised to see how quickly my personal box of apples filled up, in what seemed to be so little labor. At the end of the event, it was awesome to see the sheer number of apples we were able to pick. In an event planned to be two hours, we managed to fill all our boxes in forty-five minutes. This project served me as yet another reminder of the ease of service in the presence of positive energy."

If having a positive impact on CeDaniel and Cole was the only good thing to come out of the Low Hanging Fruit project, it still would have been worth it. But I know that every other student who joined us that day, and the many more who have gone gleaning for a cause since then, also benefited from it. I also know that the 750 pounds of apples that we gathered just on that first session helped nourish just as many people in need. And that was just the beginning. The team has big plans to expand the program next year, and there's no reason it can't serve as a model for other farms around the country and across the globe, the same way BPI is helping incarcerated people across fourteen nations and six continents.

This is the beauty of the ripple effect. You never know how far it will carry. All that's needed is for someone to start it in motion. What is your next ripple? The answer to that question is right there in front of all of us, just waiting for us to change our lens and see it.

Chapter Nine

BELIEVE IN YOURSELF, BELIEVE IN THE TEAM

always end my Vision Training for Life workshops with a session on confidence. On the playing field and in life, there is no greater predictor of success than an unwavering belief in your own abilities. In driving this point home, I like to open this part of the workshop with the Fosbury flop.

If you're a fan of track and field, you may have heard the story before. It's about an American high jumper named Dick Fosbury who revolutionized his sport by not just seeing a better way to jump high in the air, but also by having enough self-assurance to push past the naysayers. Here's how it all went down—or up, as it were.

As a high school track athlete in Oregon in the 1960s, Fosbury struggled with the high jump event because he found the traditional straddle-roll technique awkward and complicated. In this early method of jumping, athletes would cross the bar face down with their legs straddling it. Every time Fosbury tried to clear five feet, the minimum qualifying height for most high school track meets, he'd clip the bar and send it falling to the mat below.

Fosbury was an astute observer of the sport and also had a crystal-clear understanding of his own body and abilities. During his sophomore year in 1963, at a meet in Grants Pass, Oregon, he once again dislodged the bar on a straddle-roll jump. The next time up, he decided to take the unconventional approach of jumping with his back to the bar, raising his hips, and kicking his legs up in the air. He cleared five feet on that first jump and soared as high as five feet ten inches on subsequent attempts that day.

With that, the "Fosbury flop" was born, though it wouldn't be dubbed that until a year later when a newspaper covering a local track meet ran a photo with a caption that read, "Fosbury Flops Over Bar." The writer went further in the article, noting that Fosbury's high jump looked like "a fish flopping in a boat."

In fact, Fosbury was mocked pretty mercilessly at first for his unorthodox approach to the high jump. Fortunately, his innovation was matched by a steely inner confidence and he was able to ignore the many snickers and jeers. But then in 1965 he enrolled at Oregon State University, where the coach insisted Fosbury return to the straddle-roll method. Fosbury gave in at first, in a deference to his experienced college coach. Eventually, though, after his performance plateaued, his coach permitted him to return to the flop. At his first meet of the 1968 season, he flopped to an OSU record by clearing six feet ten inches. His coach stopped trying to pressure him after that.

Fosbury's meteoric rise continued when he was named to the U.S. Olympic Team competing at the 1968 Games in Mexico City.

Even then, his technique was ridiculed by many of the coaches and athletes on hand, though fans ate it up. As the high jump event got underway, Fosbury silenced critics once and for all by jumping 7 feet 4.25 inches, breaking the world record and securing a gold medal for his country before an international television audience. Today, every high jumper in the world uses the "Fosbury flop" because a sixteen-year-old had the perception to try something different, the persistence to continue, and the confidence to believe in himself.

Finding Your Confidence Core

Confidence is a state of mind. I think we can all agree on that. In one study of fourteen elite athletes (each had either medaled in a world championship, World Cup, or Olympic Games or held a world record in their respective sport), researchers asked a series of questions designed to identify the connection between confidence and cognitive behavior. The study concluded that confident athletes are better at maintaining focus and processing information. They approach competition with a far more positive mindset too—for example, perceiving pregame jitters as a sign of excitement and anticipation, rather than a lack of preparation or other negative causation. All this enables them to execute skills and strategies more successfully, leading to improved performance and medal-worthy results.

The power of confidence is clear. The harder question is: How do you enter that state of mind and stay there on a consistent basis? Having come this far in the book, I hope you're thinking that the answer must have something to do with the Five Ps. Right you are!

The more I learned about the life of Dick Fosbury, the more I realized that his confidence is an extraordinary validation of this point. The single most formative moment in Fosbury's life was also a hugely tragic one. When he was fourteen years old, he and his younger brother, Greg, just ten at the time, were out riding their bikes at dusk when a drunk driver struck and killed Greg. The tragedy devastated Fosbury's family and led to the breakup of his parents' marriage, all of which Fosbury had no choice but to bear witness to. He was consumed by grief and, as the older brother, felt responsible for Greg's death.

As Fosbury started to process the unimaginable tragedies he'd perceived, he knew he had to find some way out of his grief. Sport offered a respite. It couldn't bring his brother back or reunite his family, but it could provide an anchor of meaning in his otherwise forlorn world. Sport became his plan, the third P, and it's one of the bravest examples I've ever encountered in four decades of Vision Training. To have the courage to confront his grief in such a public and highly competitive manner took real guts. Then came the performance phase, which we know was filled with adversity at first, as Fosbury struggled with the straddle-roll technique. By this point, however, the high jump had become imbued with deep purpose, inspired as it was by his brother's death. This gave Fosbury the confidence to persist, leading to the first Fosbury flop at the age of sixteen and the many successes that followed.

It would have been easy for Fosbury to shut down in the face of so much tragedy. You can imagine others in similar situations losing interest in school, fading from society, and maybe even turning to drugs and alcohol for an escape. Fosbury chose another path. Of course, his trials and triumphs predated Vision Training by a couple decades. But I still love to share his story because it shows how maintaining clear and consistent focus makes it possible to move through life with confidence and self-belief, overcoming the highest hurdles in the process.

The Confidence Contagion

Confidence and belief do more than improve your own chances for self-fulfillment. They also have a positive impact on everyone around you. It's what I call the confidence contagion, and Vision Training for Life is a way to promote the spread of positivity, since it trains you to recognize the impact your actions have on others. A fascinating study by researchers out of Australia showed the extent to which this is true. The participants in the study were Belgian soccer players between the ages of twelve and seventeen who believed they were taking part in a soccer competition to identify the top players in the country. In other words, the talent level was as high as the stakes. The players were split into four groups and assigned a leader, introduced as the team captain, who would take them through two drills over the forty-five-minute exhibition. One drill was designed around passing, the other around shooting and dribbling.

As the drills got underway, the team captains followed a script that was designed to show high, neutral, or low confidence in the team and individual players. High-confidence captains displayed positive body language and used phrases like "Great passing; keep it going!" and "Nice ball control!" Neutral-confidence captains stood motionless throughout the session and said very little. Low-confidence captains were demonstrably negative toward their players, with slumped shoulders and critical feedback, uttering things like, "I don't call this soccer anymore; this is hopeless," and "With this team we can never win this contest. Do we really have to keep on playing?"

After the drills, players were given a survey that measured their assessment of their individual performance and that of the team, as well as their sense of identity with the team. Even though the players were equally skilled, those who were led by a high-confidence captain scored measurably higher on every single assessment. They believed they played well, they were pleased with the group performance, and they were happy to be a part of the team. To quote the study, "A leader's expressions of elevated confidence spilled over into team members' own confidence while their expressions of diminished confidence compromised team members' confidence. In contrast, when leader's confidence was neither high nor low, there was no change in team members' confidence."

Confidence is contagious. Using the tools of Vision Training, you can become more attuned to this fact, and the result will be a virtuous cycle. The more confidence you show, the more confident those around you will be, which in turn will enhance your belief in yourself further, and on and on.

In psychology, this phenomenon is known as the Pygmalion effect, referring to the work of two American psychologists named Robert Rosenthal and Lenore Jacobson. It centered on an experiment at an elementary school where students took intelligence pretests. Rosenthal and Jacobson then told the class teachers which students were in the top 20 percentile, noting their "unusual potential for intellectual growth." In fact, these students were chosen at random, with no relation to the initial test. When Rosenthal and Jacobson tested the students eight months later, they found that the randomly selected students who teachers thought would blossom scored significantly higher than their classmates.

We can think of the Pygmalion effect as a self-fulfilling prophecy, whereby a person's or a group's expectation of another person or group serves to actually bring about the prophesied behavior. I will never forget being a twelve-year-old boy and listening to Dido, my Ukrainian grandfather, in his cozy apartment in Queens, NY, as he recounted the danger and fear he and my father had faced while fleeing Ukraine, and miraculously surviving Stalin's atrocities. Suddenly, he looked me square in the eye and said, "Synok, you are going to be president someday." I laughed, taking it for a joke. His countenance turned even more serious, his stare more probing. He leaned closer to me and repeated the words, "Synok . . . you are going to be president someday." In an instant, I realized he was being completely serious. "Wow," I thought to myself. My grandfather, a man I was in awe of, really believed in me. Obviously, I didn't go on to become president, but it was a seminal moment in my young life where my grandfather's high expectations filled me with a confidence and belief that's been there ever since.

A Young Man Named Muji

As a Ukrainian, early 2022 was a dark time in my life, with the prospect of a second major invasion by Russia looking more and more likely. By February, Vladimir Putin had sent some two hundred thousand Russian troops to the Ukrainian border. As the media reported at the time, Putin claimed the massive buildup was merely a military exercise, but Western intelligence suspected it was a precursor to a Russian incursion. On the morning of February 24, those suspicions were confirmed by unprovoked Russian airstrikes carried out against cities across Ukraine.

Two days later, I was standing in the Chapel of the Holy Innocents on Bard's campus, where a student-organized vigil for Ukraine was being held. In moments of anguish, it's critical to seek out community, so that was my intention that night, to be around people who were hurting as badly as I was. One by one, students, faculty, and other members of the community got up to share words of support for the besieged people of Ukraine.

With the pandemic still raging, we were all in masks, so I closed my eyes and let the voices wash over me. At a certain point, I heard one of the speakers say that he was from Afghanistan. I opened my eyes to the sight of a young man with a slender build and big brown eyes. Even with the mask and layers of winter clothing, I could sense the confidence and positivity emanating from within him. I leaned in as he continued to speak.

"Because I am from Afghanistan," he continued, "I want to say how much I appreciate the way Ukraine has helped so many Afghan refugees over the years. If I could return the favor to the Ukrainians, I would do anything."

His message was so genuine and heartfelt. I was really struggling that week, so his words hit me like a ton of bricks. By the time he finished his speech, he was in tears, as were many in the audience. You could have heard a pin drop in the chapel. I was welling up also. I walked over to the young man and gave him a hug.

"Thank you," I said. "I can't tell you how much your words mean to me."

I wasn't planning to speak that night, but I was so inspired by the Afghani student that I made my way to the podium next. I told the supporters about my parents' escape from Stalinist Ukraine during World War II, refugees who fled through Czechoslovakia and Austria and eventually, after the war was over, made their way to Germany, which had formed camps that served as safe havens for displaced people.

"As we just heard from the brave young man from Afghanistan, Ukrainians have always been there when others needed our help. I'm so grateful that you are all here tonight for the people of Ukraine. We desperately need your love and support, now more than ever."

I was one of the last speakers that night. As the vigil wrapped up and supporters filed out of the chapel, I looked around for the young Afghani, but he was nowhere to be found. I thought of him as I lay in bed that night, and the next morning when I woke up and went through my gratitude ritual, his words were the first thing I gave thanks for.

A few weeks later, I was in my office getting ready for the official kickoff of the spring practice season. I was going through my notes when I came across one I made back in January, after a cafeteria chat I had with Dylan Kotlowitz, one of my sophomore standouts.

"Hey, Coach, me and a few of the guys were having a kick-around the other night and this international student joined in, from the Middle East, I think," Dylan had said. "Man, he was cooking us with his skills. You gotta look him up."

I jotted down his name, Mujtaba Naqib, and promised to send him a note when we got closer to the start of the season. Back in my office, I found Mujtaba's name in the college directory and sent him an email inviting him in for a quick meeting. A few days later, Mujtaba walked into my office.

"Hey, nice to meet you," I said, extending a hand.

"And it's nice to *see* you again, Coach," he said with a wry smile, shaking my hand.

My synchronicity radar is pretty on-target, but for a split second I had no idea who this person was who supposedly knew me. But then my lens shifted and I was transported back to the Chapel of the Holy Innocents.

"Oh my gosh," I started. "With the masks that night, I never got a good look at you. It's you, the Afghan student from the vigil."

"It's me," he said. "My name is Mujtaba, but everyone calls me Muji. I hope you will do the same, especially if I'm going to be the newest member of your football team."

We were both in tears, a beautiful combination of joy and sorrow and, above all, solidarity. I already knew that Muji was a special kid. Now that the universe had conspired to bring us together, I couldn't wait to discover the full depths of that specialness.

Right now, you might be thinking to yourself, "Sweet story, but what does this all have to do with confidence and belief?" It's a fair question. By way of an answer, I want to pivot for a moment and talk more about the fifth P: Persistence. As I talked about earlier in the book, the Five Ps are in constant interplay, working as one to bring about the desired effect. The process is more of a cycle than a step-by-step, so there's no real hierarchy of importance within the Five Ps. And yet, I do always say it's the first and last Ps that matter most. Perceiving is what keeps our lens wide, deep, and bright. Persistence, meanwhile, is what pushes us forward.

In the context of confidence and belief, persistence steps up as the most vital P of them all. I like to think of persistence as confidence in motion. When we believe fully in ourselves, we are able to push through every challenge and hardship. We can tap into reserves of strength and conviction that sit well beneath the surface during times of diffidence and self-doubt. In short, persistence lets us achieve our goals and become the best versions of ourselves.

TJ's Tips: Becoming Persistent Through Vision Training

So how do we maintain persistence on a consistent basis? The operative word there is "consistent." It's not enough to have bursts of persistence, followed by periods of idleness and distraction. Of course, we all need to recover and recharge. But when it comes to achieving the goals that matter most to you, whether its excellence on the playing field or fulfillment at work or within your family, total focus is essential. Here are three keys to maintaining that mindset.

Key #1: See It, Believe It

Visualization, as you might expect, is one of the core strategies for building persistence and confidence. After all, it hinges on vision, even if it's only in your mind's eye. Visualization is the act of conditioning your brain for successful outcomes. Think of it as a mental rehearsal. Sports psychologists have been studying the impact of visualization for decades and have shown repeatedly that athletes who use imagery enhance their performance at the cognitive, behavioral, and emotional level.

To show the power of visualization, I like to tell the story of Brice Merwine, one of my forwards at LIU in 2013. He had been a high-scoring machine out of central Pennsylvania, but that first season with us he underperformed by only netting a pair of goals. Then in the offseason he fractured his foot playing pickup basketball, forcing him to miss the spring training season. Suffice it to say, we did not have the highest hopes for Brice entering the 2014 campaign. But he made believers of us all by scoring twelve goals, good for third in the nation, and leading the Blackbirds back to the

Northeast Conference Tournament, all the while maintaining a 3.95 grade point average as a mathematics major, which was good enough for Academic All-American honors.

After the season ended, I met with Brice in my office for a recap. We chatted about the season and his plans for the future and then I asked the question that was most on my mind.

"In all my years of coaching, I don't think I've ever witnessed such a complete and total turnaround," I began. "How did you do it, Brice?"

"After my first year with you here at LIU, I was really down," Brice said. "Then the injury kept me out of the game for all those months. I was lost. My dad used to film all my games in high school. At some point he sent me the videos. I spent the entire summer watching myself play at the highest club level. I studied the goals I scored, my movement off the ball, even the mistakes I made and what I should have done differently. By the time the fall season came around, the moment I stepped on the field, I was able to visualize what I needed to do for you and the team."

Through the power of visualization, Brice rediscovered the player he once was and knew he could become again. Whatever your goals in life, visualization can help you reach them. There's even research showing that the technique can actually rewire the brain by firing off neurons and activating the motor cortex. The mere act of imagining an action builds connections in the brain that can lead to the same outcome in real life.

Key #2: Talk the Talk

Another of my favorite aphorisms, often attributed to Henry Ford, goes like this: Whether you think you can, or you think you can't—you're right. It gets to the heart of "self-talk" or the steady stream of thoughts and internal dialogue that's coursing through our minds at all times. It's almost impossible to shut down self-talk, so the goal is to amplify the positive thoughts while shutting out the negative ones.

I share many strategies with my athletes and students for turning self-talk into smart-talk, or a mindset that constantly has you thinking that you can. I tell them to focus on the present, not the past or the future, since the present is the only time we can act. It's also important to focus on the things you can control and forget about the things you can't. Finally, learn to separate your performance from your self-worth. Your value as a human being has nothing to do with how you perform as a student or an athlete.

Self-talk is also vital to accessing your optimal performance mode, whatever the challenge at hand might be, from running in a race to delivering a speech. Here's where repetition comes in. By repeating positive thoughts in your mind, they eventually harden into self-belief. This often takes the form of a phrase or mantra that's repeated before high-pressure performances. As a Division I volleyball player in college, early in my career, I was the libero, a defensive position in which my main job was to handle serves and dig out blistering spikes and tee up my teammates with clean passes. Anytime I would miss a play, I would say to myself, "Next one is good." It was my way of preventing negative thoughts from creeping in and sparking a string of bad passes. And guess what, the next pass was consistently good.

Michael Phelps, the greatest swimmer of all time (at least by medal count, with his twenty-eight podium visits across five Olympic Games), was famous for motivational self-talk, which he took to an almost ritualistic level. Before each meet, he would play the same Lil Wayne song, "I'm Me." The music and lyrics coaxed Phelps into a relaxed state, which he stayed in as he made his way to the starting block. Right before the race, he would slap his arms hard across his chest two or three times and say his mantra to himself: *Swim like hell.* He would always think the words, rather than say them out loud, to avoid generating too much excitement at the outset of the race. Somewhere around the halfway point of every race, he would then unleash his inner beast by repeating the mantra over and over in his head: swim like hell, swim like hell, swim like hell. That's what he did, and more often than not, it propelled him to the finish line ahead of the pack.

Like everything, self-talk is a technique that takes time and practice to perfect. But by putting the voices inside your head to work for you, listening closely to the positive thoughts and shutting out the negative ones, you will build confidence and the power to persevere.

Key # 3: Find Your Champions

Visualization and self-talk both come from within. This final motivator looks outward to the people in your life who propel you forward. There's a quote from the writer Edmund Lee that captures the importance of this so perfectly for me that I now include it in my email signature box. It goes like this: "Surround yourself with the dreamers and the doers, the believers and thinkers, but most of all, surround yourself with those who see the greatness within you, even when you don't see it yourself."

Decades of research confirm the unique role peer relationships play in our early years, especially through adolescence, where falling in with the right crowd can result in so many positive outcomes, from mental and physical health to higher levels of satisfaction in work and romantic relationships. We all know where the wrong can lead you.

Peer relationships are no less critical in adulthood, especially when it comes to maintaining resilience and perseverance. We all need people in our lives who see our greatness and encourage us to keep driving forward. These connections don't just happen, though. You need to discover and cultivate them through a constant refreshing of your lens and application of the Five Ps.

More from Muji

During that first meeting in my office with Muji, and in the weeks that followed, I learned more of his story. Having been around elite athletes most of my life, including professionals at the top of their sport, I was no stranger to displays of confidence and self-belief. Even among these paragons of perseverance, Muji was exceptional.

Though born an Afghan national, Muji spent most of his childhood in Malaysia, which his parents fled to in 1980 after the Soviet invasion of Afghanistan. Muji always longed to visit his homeland. In the summer of 2021, when the COVID-19 pandemic forced his university coursework in computer science back in Malaysia to become all virtual, his parents finally relented and let him return to live with relatives. The first six weeks were a wonderful homecoming, as Muji reconnected with family and friends and experienced the culture that coursed through his veins.

The first sign of trouble happened in the middle of July, when a roadside bomb exploded at a market he and his friends had been at not five minutes earlier.

"I'd never experienced anything like that," Muji told me. "I was in a state of shock for the next two days. But even then, despite rumors of a Taliban takeover, life returned to normal."

Then came August 15. The morning began like any other. Muji woke up, got dressed, and made his way to the breakfast hall. He was living in government housing as part of an internship with a U.S.-backed agency that provides protection and support for Afghans seeking sanctuary outside the country. It was not the kind of work the Taliban looked kindly on.

As soon as he walked outside, a friend ran up to Muji and told him to throw anything he needed into a bag and get out of there. With his laptop, documents, and the clothes on his back, he laid low at the home of a relative in the area, as the Taliban rolled into Kabul and took control of the capital city.

It's an unimaginable situation for most seventeen-year-olds to think of, essentially in a foreign land and a presumed enemy of one of the world's most feared terrorist organizations. Instead of cowering in fear, Muji contacted his supervisor at the agency.

"Let me come to the office," he said. "I can help get our people out while there's still time. Many of them can't do it on their own."

His supervisor agreed and Muji spent the next nine days at his office, helping staff there complete the paperwork they would need to be granted sanctuary status and leave the country. It wasn't high-level officials he helped, but rather the janitors and cooks and cleaners who lacked the education and computer skills to fill out the forms on their own.

"I knew that if the Taliban came into the building, I would probably be killed on the spot," Muji recalled. "Not only was I working with the Americans, I'm of Hazaras ethnicity and the Taliban are predominantly Pashtun. I wouldn't have had a chance. But I also knew it was the right thing to do. If I was going to die, at least it would be with honor, knowing I had helped as many people as I could."

This went on for more than a week. Finally, every Afghan staffer had their papers. Only then did Muji make his way to Kabul airport and the scene of absolute chaos that was described in many media reports at the time. He was at the airport when a massive explosion killed more than one hundred Afghans and thirteen U.S. soldiers.

"I was so tired and terrified at that point," Muji said. "There were many moments when I wanted to give up, but I reminded myself how far I had come in life and that this was just one more hurdle to overcome."

Through perseverance and good fortune, Muji made it onto one of the last rescue flights out of Kabul. He was evacuated first to Qatar, where he lived under a tent for four days with seven hundred other refugees. Then, without notice, he was transported to an encampment in Germany, where he lived for forty-five days with about 1,200 displaced people. Though he was relatively safe, life was still a struggle. There were no showers in either camp, so he resorted to cleaning his body and clothes with hand sanitizer, which, thanks to the pandemic, was in abundant supply. There was no internet, either, but he persuaded an American soldier at the German encampment to lend him his hot spot so that he could get a message back to his parents in Malaysia.

Otherwise, it was a period of interminable waiting around. To pass the time, Muji recorded video diary entries on his phone, describing his situation and his will to push through the uncertainty. After nearly six weeks in Germany, an official entered his room one morning and told him he was on the next flight to the U.S. Muji had always wanted to visit America, but he never could have imagined it happening under these circumstances.

Muji landed in Philadelphia and immediately boarded a bus for Quantico, the Marine base camp in Virginia that provided temporary housing for thousands of Afghan refugees before they were resettled elsewhere in the U.S. Muji's fate was up in the air, so immediately upon arrival at the base he began searching for scholarship opportunities, encouraged by something his father had told him during their first phone call. "Coming from a country that has been persecuted for so long, you must never take education for granted," his father had said. Muji also believed in his abilities. "If anyone deserved a scholarship, it was me," he said. There was no arrogance to his words, no sense of entitlement. He simply believed that the challenges he had overcome made him uniquely qualified for a chance to excel at higher education.

It was Muji's sister who alerted him to the scholarship program at Bard. It was intended for students from the American University of Afghanistan in Kabul, which Muji wasn't, but he applied anyway, even making a two-minute video describing his experiences from the last few months. A few days later, he had a call from the admissions department saying he had been accepted into the program.

Muji arrived at the Bard campus on January 11, 2021. It was very difficult at first. In the middle of class that first week, a loud boom from construction work happening outside triggered a PTSD panic attack that lasted the entire day. He returned to his room that night and cried himself to sleep. When he woke up the next morning, he vowed to make a change.

"I told myself that I can't keep doing this," he said. "I need to get up and do well in my studies. That's why I am here and that's what will bring me one step closer to my goals." Later that evening, he heard a bunch of guys kicking the ball around outside his dorm and decided to join in. That's what brought the remarkable Muji into my life.

After hearing Muji's whole story and reflecting deeply on it, I realized the extent to which the confidence I saw in him that night at the vigil was the product of his unshakable perseverance. And that he embodied all the strategies I talked about in my workshops. There was the use of visualization in how he envisioned the honor he would feel helping his Afghan brothers and sisters versus the dishonor of doing nothing. There was self-talk, which he took next-level by recording videos of himself at the refugee camp in Germany. And there was the way he looked to people who believed in his abilities, including his father, who motivated him to pursue his education, even in the face of enormous odds.

Muji joined the soccer team that spring. He grew up playing futsal, a small-sided version of the game, so while his ball skills are phenomenal, adjusting to the big field and 11 v. 11 play was a challenge, plus he suffered an injury during preseason that kept him sidelined for several weeks. Still, even if he didn't end up scoring a bunch of goals for us that season, he was an incredible addition to the squad. His confidence was a true contagion. The team was so inspired by his example that they used the occasion of our annual spring alumni game to fundraise for Bard's Afghan Student Fund. Fittingly, Muji scored a beautiful goal in the contest.

Muji racked up plenty of wins off the field, including stellar grades and a coveted internship with Pfizer. "I was the last of hundreds of applicants to interview for the position," Muji told me. "The interview was supposed to be thirty minutes, but it ended up being close to an hour. Later, my supervisor told me it was my goals in life that convinced them to give me the internship."

"What are your goals?" I asked, realizing I'd never heard that part of his story.

"I'm an IT guy," he answered. "I love computer science. My goal in life is to return to Afghanistan and bring the internet to as many of my people as possible."

With that answer, I realized that Muji isn't just an example of the confidence and perseverance discussed in this chapter. He embodies the whole of Vision Training. There's integrity in his desire to do the right thing. There's selflessness in his helping others. There's his constant search for purpose and meaning.

And what about passion? Every week throughout the soccer season, I give the team a different theme to reflect on based on our team ethos. I picked four players on Monday to prepare a meaningful example of the week's theme to share in the circle before training.

"As we all know, this week's ethos is Heart," Muji said to the squad when his turn came up. "The way I look at heart is when a person is there for someone through good and bad times, whether they know each other or not."

He then went on to describe his early days at Bard and the struggles he faced coming off the traumatic escape from the Taliban and his odyssey bouncing from one refugee camp to the next. He talked about the vigil for Ukraine, the connection we made that night, and the joy he felt when we reunited through the game of soccer.

"That was when I knew that the culture of the team was going to be very supportive," he told the team. "Because if Coach TJ was there to support me when we didn't even know each other, then I could only imagine the support I would receive from the coaches and the team the moment I joined the team."

It had been less than a year since the cruelty of war had cast Muji into the wilderness, a lone eighteen-year-old without family, country, or community. But he had belief in himself, the will to persevere, and the vision to see possibilities where others might have only seen darkness, including that night back in January, where he looked out onto the cold, dark campus and noticed a handful of guys knocking around a soccer ball.

"I'm going to end today's ethos by saying I love each and every one of you for making me feel included on this team, whether I'm on the field or on the bench. Kicking the ball around with all of you really helped me during my tough times, and because of all of you, I feel one thousand percent better. Thank you to everyone for being amazing, and I am very proud to be part of this community."

Changing the World, One Step at a Time

Just as I always start the confidence and belief section of my Vision Training for Life workshops with the Fosbury flop, I always close it the same way—with the starfish story. It's based on an original work called "The Star Thrower" by Loren Eiseley, a twentieth-century American writer and naturalist. Like all great oral stories, it's been told and retold so many times that the details tend to shift around some. But the central message is always the same. Here's how I like to tell the story.

One day, a young boy was walking along a beach that was strewn with starfish. They had been washed ashore by a storm the night before. Every few feet, the boy would stop, pick up a starfish, and fling it into the sea.

The boy came upon a man who looked at him with amusement.

"Little boy," the man said, "what are you doing? Look at how many starfish are on the beach. There are thousands and thousands of them. You can't possibly save all the starfish. You can't possibly make a difference."

The boy looked up at the man. He bent down and picked up the largest starfish he could find. He waded into the water, leaned back, and with all his might tossed it forward and watched as it disappeared into the sea.

He then turned and said, "I just made a difference for that one."

All you have to do is make a difference with one. This is the essence of Vision Training. It doesn't happen all at once. For the players I coach, the first check of their shoulder doesn't unlock the mystery of the game. But it gives them the sliver of a view on which to build. Weeks and months and years of eyes-up play go by before they start to see the entirety of the field and realize their full potential as players.

The same is true for Vision Training for Life. Applying the Five Ps doesn't happen overnight. Through small changes that you implement every day, your lens becomes wider, deeper, and brighter. You find gratitude in the little things. Your sense of purpose grows. Your connections expand and deepen. It's one starfish at a time.

Chapter Ten

SEE BEYOND THE GAME

As you begin to incorporate the Five Ps and Three Ls of Vision Training, your lens on the world and your place in it will become wider, brighter, and deeper. In sports, we talk about players taking their game to the next level. In life, the expanded perspective has an even more profound impact. It enables you to find and live your purpose and meaning that you otherwise may have missed. One of my favorite quotes, attributed to Confucius, goes like this: "We have two lives, and the second begins when we realize we only have one." Vision Training is a way to make this realization and live your best life.

The Confucius quote was actually sent to me by a former player named Robert Black, the third-string goalie at Appalachian State, where I spent a single year as head coach in 1998. I'd been brought in to revive a Division I program that for many years had withered on the vine. I'll never forget walking into the meeting room that first day and telling this group of athletic, highly skilled players that I was going to take them back to the fundamentals of soccer and show them a new way to play the game. There were several top players on the team, some on full scholarships who were All-Americans in high school and All-Conference players many times over during their careers at App. And that first day of training I had them doing technical passing and receiving exercises that incorporated vision and decision-making.

The Mountaineers had been kicked around enough in recent years in the competitive Southern Conference that they were open to anything. I had to work hard to earn their trust from the beginning. "I know how talented and athletic and motivated you all are," I said during that first team meeting. "I'm here to help us all get better together."

The transition was helped by the fact that we had a bunch of stellar personalities on the team, none more so than Robert, whom everyone called Bert. He was that special combination of funny, smart, and warm, the kind of guy that lit up any room he walked into, including our locker room. I'd often come in and see him regaling the guys with a colorful tale, delivered in his deep, southern drawl, or pumping the team up with words of encouragement before a big match. He kept everyone loose. Every team needs a guy like Bert.

Bert's actual ability as a player was another story, though not for lack of effort. He'd been a late bloomer in high school and came to Appalachian with high hopes of continuing to flourish. Unfortunately, a series of injuries and academic mishaps sidelined him for much of his first three years (talk about hard luck; in Bert's junior year, after battling back from a pulmonary embolism, he was deemed ineligible after the school's compliance officer forgot to tell the NCAA that he had switched majors).

Bert's senior year was when I took over the program. Though I quickly recognized his importance to the culture of the team, I hadn't seen him as a starter. Another senior keeper won the job, and I had also brought in a lights-out freshman to serve as our number two, though I never stated this explicitly to Bert or the team. I practice full transparency with my players, but I also believe there's no point in needlessly creating drama or tension. Everyone knew who our starting keeper was. As long as he was healthy and getting the job done, at that point in time, the question of backups was moot.

Then, with a few games left in the season, fate intervened when our keeper collided with the opposition's striker and got the worst of it, in the form of multiple broken bones and torn ligaments in his hand. As he was aided off the field by our training staff, Bert jumped up from the bench and started getting loose.

I signaled for the freshman. It was a tough decision, but I'd of course been preparing in my mind for this scenario the entire season. I simply felt that going with the freshman would benefit the program in both the short and long term. Bert took a seat back down on the bench. He didn't say a word, but he didn't have to. His body language spoke volumes. He was pissed. I realized I had dropped the ball by not communicating my plan to him earlier in the season.

The next morning he marched into my office in his street clothes. I closed the door behind him, pulled my chair in front of the desk, and asked him to take a seat on the sofa.

"What's the plan here, Coach?" Bert asked, skipping any pleasantries. "Because I have to tell you, I was pretty surprised by your decision yesterday. I'm a senior. I've worked my tail off all year. It's my turn. This is my time."

There was a lot of emotion in the room, so I took a deep breath to allow for some of it to diffuse. I then apologized for not sharing my plans with him sooner. I knew that I needed to create space in the moment. After a few seconds of silence, I told Bert that my plan was to stick with the freshman.

"Well, if that's your decision, then I quit," Bert said sharply.

Again I let his words hang there for a few seconds. It was important to maintain the space. Then I told Bert that I thought that would be a mistake.

"You're an incredibly valuable member of this team, Bert," I told him. "In the locker room, on the training pitch, in the huddle, the guys look up to you. I know you're upset right now. But I would encourage you to take a day and really think this through."

Bert was still mad as hell, but he agreed to give it a day. We both stood up from our chairs. We'd only known each other for a handful of months, but there was a deep well of respect and admiration between us. "Remember, Bert," I said. "You can change what you face or you can change the way you face it." As he walked out of my office, I honestly wasn't sure if I was seeing Bert for the last time.

He wasn't at training the next day. His absence left a gaping hole in the squad, and the energy at practice was noticeably low. So you can imagine the collective sigh the following day when Bert ambled into the locker room and started lacing up his boots.

"What are y'all looking at?" he barked. "We got Georgia Southern in two days. Let's go!" Bert was back.

It was a good thing too, because, wouldn't you know it, with ten minutes left in the half against Georgia Southern, our freshman keeper took out a player outside of the box and earned an immediate red card, which carried a two-game suspension. Bert jumped up again from the bench. This time it really was his turn.

We ended up losing the match, which meant a few days later we'd have to travel three hours to Statesboro, Georgia, to face GSU once again in the first round of the conference tournament. I'll never forget that bus ride. It was a monsoon the whole way down, which I couldn't help but see as an omen. Besides the fact that GSU had dominated us for years, we were missing several key players, including our starting sweeper and center mid. And, of course, starting in goal was our third-string keeper.

The rain finally let up a few hours before kickoff, but the pitch was still soaked to the core with the ball skipping all over the place. However, I could read the confidence in Bert's body language as our guys took the field. Not two minutes in, their striker collected the ball at the edge of the box and ripped a shot at the top corner.

Then I watched in amazement as Bert sprang through the air, his lumbering frame in full extension, and got enough of the ball to parry it over the crossbar. It was one of the finest saves I'd seen all season. On the ensuing corner kick, GSU played a lofting ball into the box. Bert got there first, but the wet ball slipped through his gloves and bounced toward the far post. Once again, he sprang for the ball and reached it just as one of their guys was about to smash it into the bottom of the goal. Bert made the stop. It was game on.

Bert would later tell me that this was the first and only time in his athletic career that he truly felt in the zone. He was clearly performing in the flow state. "I knew what they were going to do with the ball before they did," he said to me. It was true. Bert was absolutely lights out. I'd never seen anything quite like it.

With about eight minutes left, we finally broke the scoreless draw with a breakaway goal by our star freshman striker, Jordy Broder, who buried his league-leading thirteenth goal of the year. In the waning seconds of the match, their star forward got through one-on-one with Bert. As he'd done all day, Bert read the play perfectly and stuffed the guy. A few heartbeats later, the whistle blew. We had beaten Georgia Southern.

Our entire bench went running to the freshman who had scored the game winner. That's soccer—all the glory to the goal scorers. I headed the other way to Bert, who had fallen to his knees on the muddy turf. I pulled him to his feet and gave him the biggest bear hug I could manage.

"I'm so proud of you Bert, so, SO proud of you!" I repeated over and over, until the rest of the squad arrived to celebrate the true man of the match.

I'll come back to Bert's story later in the chapter to show how this formative moment helped him find deeper meaning in his life decades down the line. But even without that later payoff, Bert had already benefited from the values of Vision Training by choosing to find opportunity in adversity. It would have been very easy for him to walk away from the game after hearing my decision to start our freshman keeper over him. Instead, he shifted his perspective on the situation, doubled down on his role as locker room leader, and chose a path of persistence.

The Search for Meaning

During my final few years at LIU, as I was just beginning with the Five Ps and Vision Training for Life, I started running a book club with my team over the winter. I'd give every player a title to read while they were home on break and then we'd gather during the first week of the semester for group discussions. As you've heard me say, Vision Training is about gathering information. On the soccer field, this is accomplished through eyes-up, head-on-a-swivel play.

In life, reading is one of the best ways to learn and grow. "Yes, TJ, no kidding," I'm certain you're thinking.

Point taken! But it's also true that reading rates are way down from years past, thanks in large part to the many distractions of social media. A 2021 Gallup Poll found that American adults are reading two to three fewer books per year than they did between 2001 and 2016. The decline is particularly steep among college graduates. According to the same poll, they read six fewer books on average in 2021 than they did between 2002 and 2016. So, yes, anything I can do to get my players off their phones and into a book is energy well spent.

Of course, there are other sources of rich, constructive content out there, including podcasts. One of my current favorites is *One Step Beyond* with Aram Arslanian, a podcast about transformation through leadership. Aram has conversations with people who are creating change in business, in their community, and in their lives by choosing to lead. It's about daring to overcome barriers, push past limitations, and reshape our present and our future. I encourage you to check it out. Although I haven't owned a TV for many years, I know there's a lot of quality content there as well.

But reading will always be my number one form of information gathering, because it requires a focus and commitment that's missing in other forms of media. For my book clubs, I've tried a few different titles over the years, but the one that's had the most impact by far is *Man's Search for Meaning*, a 1946 book by Viktor Frankl about his experiences in a Nazi concentration camp during World War II.

Part autobiography, part psychological treatise, *Man's Search for Meaning* is a hard, harrowing read, with some very dark and disturbing passages. But it's also a story of inspiration, since Frankl shows how his ability to find and maintain meaning in life, despite the unthinkable horrors happening around him, allowed him to survive the ordeal. As he puts it in the book, "Those who have a 'why' to live, can bear with almost any 'how.'" Every time my teams get together to talk about the book, I can see and hear Frankl's message resonate with the guys.

"I was so angry at the start of winter break because I pulled a C in Physics Lab," I remember one player saying, after we broke out into small groups. "I thought I'd done at least B work this semester and it really made me mad. But as I got deeper into the book, I realized there's something more than grades and how many goals I score this season. I don't know what it is exactly, but I know I need to shift my lens to find it."

One of the most satisfying feelings is when my players or students take the language of Vision Training and apply it to their life. *Man's Search for Meaning* is one of the best tools I've discovered for jump-starting this process. In another favorite passage, Frankl talks about the link between meaning and self-determination. He writes: "Everything can be taken from a man but one thing: the last of the human freedoms—to choose one's attitude in any given set of circumstances, to choose one's own way; to choose how you will respond to the situation. You cannot control what happens to you in life but you can always control what you feel and do about what happens to you. Any man can, even under such circumstances, decide what shall become of him—mentally. It is this spiritual freedom—which cannot be taken away—that makes life meaningful and purposeful."

This is such an important takeaway and it's become foundational to Vision Training for Life. Remember my meeting with Bert in the coach's room at Appalachian State when he was ready to quit the team? "Change what you face or change the way you face it," I told him. Regardless of what's happening in your life—with school or work, with your health, with your relationships—you have the freedom to respond however you want. It's in your responses that the deepest meaning of life often lies. I and the rest of his teammates are deeply thankful that Bert chose to "change the way he faced it" and came back to lead our team in the playoffs.

Finding Meaning in Adversity

In the framework of Vision Training, adversity is a chance to process and plan—the second and third Ps in the Five Ps. Picture the playing field: After battling hard for forty-five minutes, a team concedes a goal just before the half. How does the team respond? How do they formulate a plan to avoid adversity and find success?

I'll always remember that frigid night in January of 2013, lying in bed fully clothed plus a winter coat and hat, staring up at the ceiling of the nine-hundred-square-foot apartment on the Jersey coast that was my new home. After twenty-two years, my marriage had come to a sudden and unexpected end. As anyone who has been through a divorce can attest, the details don't matter all that much, especially not a decade later. But that first night was brutal. My daughters were sixteen and nineteen at the time, so mine had been a highly active homelife, not some lonely empty nest. Adding insult to injury, a storm was clobbering the East Coast at the time, so the apartment was without power; hence the extra layers of clothing to fend off the freezing temperatures.

I could have wallowed in it, and the truth is I was depressed for many weeks. But I knew this was also an opportunity to change my life for the better. As a coach and an educator, I'd always found purpose by serving others, but I made the decision to double down on that mission. Thinking back on that time, I now realize it was the true beginning of Vision Training for Life. It was the moment when I began applying the lessons of the soccer field to real life. I would not be where I am today, writing these words, if my marriage hadn't fallen apart.

A few weeks after that dark, frigid night of the soul in my new bachelor pad, I was out on the equally frozen streets of New York City with my LIU team. We were taking part in a service project that happens annually in the city called HOPE NYC, short for Homeless Outreach Population Estimate. Over the course of a single night, volunteers canvass streets, subway stations, parks, and other public spaces across the city to identify individuals living unsheltered. I saw this as an opportunity to broaden my guys' perspective—and my own too.

We interacted with maybe a dozen unhoused people that night and persuaded three of them to get onto the van that would take them to shelter. One of the successes was led by a quiet young man from Arizona named Nick. I remember him cautiously approaching a man who was huddled against a city building beside a pile of his belongings. Like so many unsheltered people, the man was a war veteran. I don't know what was said between them, but after a couple minutes Nick came over and said the man was willing to take a ride. As the van pulled up and a pair of trained professionals helped the man to safety, my divorce felt like a million years ago. One of the greatest challenges in my life had given it a whole new depth of meaning. I knew everything was going to be okay.

Adversity is hard. But it is also an opportunity to grow. During challenging times, use the Five Ps of Vision Training to add depth and dimension to your awareness, and I promise you will discover things about yourself you never saw before. The great players always want to face the toughest opponents because they know that in order to be successful, they will need to elevate their game. They know the challenge will make them better. In the same way, facing adversity head-on is one of the best ways to bring deeper purpose and meaning into your life.

Finding Meaning in Mentoring

There's a host of literature on the benefits of mentoring. Mentors provide information and knowledge, they challenge you to go farther, they celebrate your wins. All of that is true, and it's part of the reason why I've always sought mentors throughout my life and also why I've happily served as a mentor for countless others. But an even bigger benefit of mentoring is the way in which it helps you find (or rediscover) meaning throughout the course of your life. That's true regardless of which side of the equation you're on. When done right, the relationship is deeply *transformational* (versus transactional) for both people.

So how do you do it right? Modern society isn't as conducive to mentorships as in the past. Think about the workplace. Back when workers stayed at the same job for most of their careers, bosses were natural mentors, because they had time to develop relationships with their employees. These days, most workers don't stay in the same job long enough for those connections to form. It's no wonder 76 percent of people say that mentors are important, but only 37 percent actually have one, according to one industry report.

You need to expand your lens to other possibilities. Look for thought leaders in your chosen field and build a relationship. Join new clubs and organizations that will allow you to connect with people who are farther along the path you hope to travel. This is an instance where social media can be a positive force—for example, allowing you to seek out and follow potential mentors on platforms like LinkedIn.

As the mentee, the goal is to find a mentor who sees something in you that you haven't yet seen in yourself. I talked earlier in the book about Norman Schwartz, who became one of my most important mentors after he recognized my potential for motivational speaking that day at a workshop on the LIU Brooklyn campus. He saw something in me that I hadn't yet seen in myself, and the impact on my life has been profound and far-reaching.

This is always my goal as a mentor. I think about Moose, a Lebanese-born refugee raised in Canada who I recruited to LIU in 2004. He was an amazing young man and a goal-scoring machine. His grades were just average, but I knew he had a good head on his shoulders. His real goal in life was to have a successful career that would allow him to help support his parents.

"What do you think you want to do?" I asked Moose during one of our early one-on-one meetings.

"I want to be a pharmacist," he said. "But I know my grades aren't—"

"You want to meet the dean of the pharmacy school?" I asked, talking over his self-doubts.

"Um, sure," Moose answered.

The next morning we were in the dean's office. Like most people, the dean took a shine to Moose, but he wasn't there to mince words.

"You'll have to make a choice between soccer and pharmacy," he said. "You can't do both. It's too much work."

"I was hoping to do both," Moose said softly.

SEE BEYOND THE GAME · 193

"Well, it's your decision," the dean said. "Just know that no one has ever done it before. You look like a nice kid and I'd hate to see you fail."

As we were walking back across campus, I could tell that Moose was feeling dejected.

"Hey, Moose," I said. "Are you ready to prove him wrong?"

A big smile filled his face. Sure enough, Moose became the first LIU NCAA Division I athlete to earn a PharmD (three more of our guys would follow in his footsteps over the next decade). Not only that, Moose continued to crush it on the soccer field, leading us to the Conference Championship in 2005 and winning the Scholar Athlete of the Year award.

Today, Moose works as a pharmacist in Michigan, where he helps support his mom and dad, as well as a family of his own. Obviously, he deserves all the credit for the years of hard work. As a mentor, all I did was help him discover the potential that was in him all along.

Finding Meaning in Community

We are all here to form human connections. One of the reasons I love soccer is that it's a free-flowing game that involves so many moving parts, with eleven players working in concert toward one collective goal. Not many sports require that level of communal effort. It's a beautiful thing.

In *Man's Search for Meaning*, Frankl talks about community in the context of love, which he calls "the ultimate and highest goal to which man can aspire." He's not speaking of romantic love, but rather the universal love that exists between any two people—friends, teammates, neighbors, colleagues, teachers, coaches, and so on. This is what I refer to as "community."

When we give ourselves to a community, we help those around us. And in the process, we discover ourselves. As Frankl puts it, "No one can become fully aware of the very essence of another human being unless he loves him. By his love he is enabled to see the essential traits and features in the beloved person; and even more, he sees that which is potential in him, which is not yet actualized but yet ought to be actualized."

Finding love and community is not a simple process. Neither one comes easily. The key is the fifth P, Persistence, which is why I think of it as the second most important one. As a coach, I get to experience this over and over with each new team. At the start of the season, it's a new group of players who have never operated as a unit. Through weeks of hard work and persistence, a community starts to form. By the end of the season, win or lose, we're a group who loves one another, and each player's life has new meaning as a result.

This is what it's all about, and Vision Training is designed to get you there. It is about seeing other people, seeing yourself, and finding the thing that connects you. Then doing it over and over until you are surrounded by love and community.

Back to Bert

A few minutes after my long, proud embrace of Bert following our stunning upset at Georgia Southern University, I was walking off the soggy field when a middle-aged guy approached me. Bert's dad, it turned out.

"Congrats on the win, Coach," he said, then added, "Robert is going to remember this experience for the rest of his life."

I keep in touch with many of my players and students. Even though I only had Bert for a year, he's been a particularly close connection in the ensuing decades. I can confirm not only that he still remembers his senior-year experience at App, but also that it's helped shape the person he is today, twenty-five years later, as it will no doubt continue to influence the person he becomes over the next quarter century and beyond. This is such an important point: our life's purpose and meaning is constantly evolving. It will look one way during young adulthood, another in middle age, and another during the twilight of life. Even from year to year, month to month, and day to day, there are microshifts in our life's purpose. Don't fear the change, which is constant in life; instead, embrace it and live your purpose.

In my Vision Training for Life workshops, I always pose this question to attendees: What's the most important moment in your life? People mention the birth of a child or their marriage day or graduating from college. Those are all special moments, I acknowledge. I share my most important moment with the audience.

"This moment," I say. "Being here in this lecture hall with you all, learning from what you have to say, working together toward a shared goal of expanding our lens on the world and our place in it. Right now, this is the most important moment in my life."

It's not just about being present, though that's clearly the first step. It's also about being intentional in your thoughts and actions. Think back to the Five Ps. Are you taking in information and making deliberate, well-informed decisions? Are you executing with purpose? And are you doing this time after time, on a consistent basis?

Here's what Frankl has to say on this in *Man's Search for Meaning*:

It did not really matter what we expected from life, but rather what life expected from us. We needed to stop asking about the meaning of life, and instead to think of ourselves as those who were being questioned by life—daily and hourly. Our answer must consist, not in talk and meditation, but in right action and in right conduct. Life ultimately means taking the responsibility to find the right answer to its problems and to fulfill the tasks which it constantly sets for each individual.

That's why it's so important to constantly refresh your lens and think about what life is asking of us. Not surprisingly, this is something Bert did—and does—extremely well.

Not long after graduation, he opened a sports marketing firm, using his ample intelligence and charisma to build a successful career consulting to the likes of Evander Holyfield, PUMA, and Kraft. He was doing very well for himself, providing a beautiful home for his wife, Sarah, and their son, Bobby, in North Carolina. But after about a decade, he started to realize that something was missing.

"I was in my midthirties when I started to really understand that I'd been floating through life, rather than living deliberately," he told me during one of the regular Zoom calls we had throughout the pandemic. "This was around the time you were building out the Five Ps and Vision Training for Life. Seeing how you were living your life, especially knowing you'd been through your own share of stuff, made me want to make changes of my own."

Bert was deep in the process of self-reflection when tragedy struck; the twelve-year-old son of his business partner died by suicide. It opened his eyes to the growing mental health epidemic affecting youth in America and around the world.

As he started to look around for direction on what to do, it came from an unlikely source: his great-grandfather and legendary golfer, Bobby Jones. The lineage had always been something of an albatross for Bert, knowing he could never achieve the same level of success. But now, instead of comparing himself to his great-grandfather, he looked to learn from his life. Reading through Jones's letters, he appreciated his namesake's character and integrity, and he also began to see how much of life was contained in the game of golf. As Jones once put it, "Golf is the closest game to the game we call life. You get bad breaks from good shots; you get good breaks from bad shots—but you have to play the ball where it lies."

In 2021, Bert started the Generation Next Project, which hosts golf-based mental wellness retreats for teens and their parents built around experiential learning, giving them the tools they need to develop positive traits, like empathy and self-awareness. The experience was nothing short of transformational. As his life took on deeper purpose and meaning, his entire outlook changed. His relationship with his family improved. His friendships expanded. He even dropped the extra thirty pounds he'd been lugging around for the last decade.

In another call, Bert talked to me about a running debate he's had with Kevin Turner, one of the best players from Bert's early years at Appalachian, and still one of his closest friends. "The argument goes like this: Would I want Kevin's career, on paper one of the top ten guys to come out of App all time, playing every game of every season. Or would I want what I had—one chance over the course of ninety minutes to make the most of it. With the wisdom of hindsight, knowing how that experience set me up to find the purpose and meaning in life that I have today, I'll take the latter every time, six days to Sunday."

As a senior at Appalachian, Bert found the game of soccer and figured out the player he was. Then he used the experience to see beyond the game and find purpose in life. Everyone's journey is their own, and there's no right or wrong way to go about it. The key is to make it with your eyes wide open and persistence in your heart. Now get out there and do it. Pick your head up, pick your **eyes up**, and live the life you always wanted, and the one that you deserve.

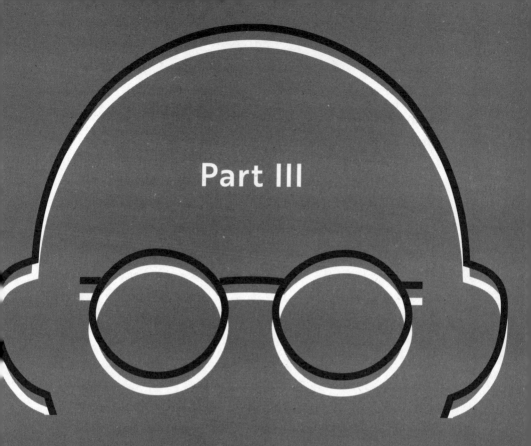

Part III

FINDING THE GOOD IN OTHERS

Chapter Eleven

ANTONIN KOSTECKY

I loved my father deeply—his kindness and sense of humor, the way he could light up a room, his ability to connect with anyone, including my friends in high school, so much so that at our fortieth class reunion they all asked about Antonin, or "Tony," as they knew him. Also, I never for a second doubted his role as provider and protector; remember, my dad was the one who insisted the doctors save my eye after it was impaled by a nail when I was twelve. But like many parent/child relationships, ours had its complications, a point that became painfully clear after his sudden passing from a heart attack when I was twenty-seven.

I was well into my coaching career at this point, a journey that had officially begun several years earlier with my decision to attend East Stroudsburg University and study physical education. This was not the path my dad had envisioned for me. Like many European immigrants from that era, having escaped so much hardship back home in order to pursue a better life in America, he put a premium on stable, prestigious, high-paying professions. As the old saying went, "You can become a doctor, a lawyer, an engineer—or a disgrace."

My father never went so far as to call me a disgrace, but he also showed little interest in my coaching life. This lack of validation always stung, because in my mind, my calling was a personal passion that allowed me to make a positive impact on others. I might not have been saving lives on the operating table, or making a ton of money on Wall Street, but through the game of soccer I was helping young people find their way in the world. Dad didn't see it that way, or if he did, he didn't let on. Then, in an instant, he was gone.

The funeral was held at St. Andrew's Ukrainian Orthodox Church in New Jersey. It was the usual gathering of friends and family, along with members of the local Ukrainian community, plus many of my father's work colleagues, most of whom I'd never met. Following the full Orthodox service, my mother, sister, and I took our positions at the front of the receiving line as a steady stream of attendees offered their condolences as they passed by my father's casket.

"You must be TJ!" a middle-aged man in a gray suit said to me warmly, maybe midway through the procession. I assumed he was an old relative who I hadn't seen in many years or maybe a loose acquaintance from the neighborhood.

"Yes, sir," I said. "Thank you for being here."

"I worked with your dad for the last ten years," the man continued. "Boy, did he love to talk about you and your soccer. It was always, 'TJ scored another goal,' or 'TJ got a scholarship,' or 'TJ became head coach.' He was so proud of you!"

"Thank you for that," I said, though in my mind I was thinking, "What a jerk. He's full of it. This guy is making up stuff about my dad just to try to make me feel better." The receiving line continued and a few minutes later, here was another middle-aged guy in a black suit beaming up at me.

"TJ! Do you know that your father kept a folder in his office with all the newspaper clippings and photos from your matches? Anytime I walked in, he insisted on showing me your latest achievement. You really made your old man proud."

Some version of this exchange happened a few more times that day, enough that I knew it wasn't part of a warped conspiracy on the part of my father's work pals to comfort me at his funeral. My father really had been proud of my life in soccer. Yet any satisfaction the revelation brought was quickly countered with this thought: "Why the hell didn't he ever tell me so himself?"

The question gnawed at me for months. It was wrapped up in my entire grieving process. In the end, I realized I could never understand my father's thinking or motivations. Even if I had the chance to ask him directly, his answers probably wouldn't make sense or bring about any resolution. Like I said earlier, the relationship between parent and child is a complicated and delicate one.

What I *could* do was learn from the experience. And here's the key takeaway I reached—that for the rest of my life, not only would I commit to using Vision Training to pick out the positive in others, I would also make darn sure they heard about everything I saw. As I developed Vision Training for Life, this idea became baked into the program and now serves as a core mantra: *Find the good in others.*

That's the idea that I want to turn to now. Through the implementation of the Seven Rules of Vision Training covered in the last section of the book, you now have all the tools you need to keep your lens wide, deep, and bright, empowering you to form deep, lasting connections in a life filled with meaning. The next step in the process is passing the power on to others. Since it uses all the same basic building blocks of Vision Training—the Five Ps, Listening and Learning, Confidence and Belief, and so on—I won't introduce you to a whole new set of rules here. Instead, I'd like to send you out with a handful of stories that show the process in action. Up first, the one about a taciturn parking garage attendant and my favorite cartoon gorilla.

Chapter Twelve

SIX STORIES OF FINDING THE GOOD IN OTHERS

The Silent Parking Garage Attendant

I was still living in New Jersey when I first joined LIU in Brooklyn, so I used to carpool in with my assistant coach, Chris Lawrence. It was a chance to shoot the breeze, talk strategy, and plan our training sessions, plus there was free parking in the campus garage.

To exit at the end of the day, we'd show our ticket and school ID to the attendant stationed in a small booth next to the boom gate. It was always the same attendant—a massive specimen of a man who seemed even bigger squeezed into the tiny booth. His eyes were always pinned to a mini portable television. As we pulled up to the booth, he'd stick out a meaty paw, swipe our ticket, and send us on our way, without so much as a grunt.

I can't resist a challenge, so from day one I did my best to engage the guy. "Hey, how's it going?" I'd say. Nothing. "How about this weather?" I'd try. Silence. "Anything good on TV?" That time he at least glanced up from the set, but only to shoot me a look that said he'd like nothing more than to beat me to a pulp.

After a few weeks of this, Chris finally had enough. "Why are you wasting your time with this dude?" he asked. "He obviously doesn't want to talk to us."

"Well, I want to talk to him," I responded. "I want to connect with him. I don't like seeing him ticked off at the end of every day. It doesn't feel good."

My desire to connect went even deeper. Despite the attendant's gruff facade, I knew there was plenty of goodness deep within that hulking frame. I was determined to find a way to unleash it. This comes back to an idea I've talked about throughout the book, that when we have the capacity to make a positive change in the world, however big or small, I believe we have an obligation to do it. This was the challenge I was locked in with the parking garage attendant.

Weeks turned to months and the routine remained the same. After a while, Chris started to ignore me, even when it was his turn to drive and I would lean across his seat to issue the day's pleasantries to the attendant.

Then one day we rolled up to the booth. I was in the driver's seat and had a clear view of the TV. There on the screen was an old cartoon from the 1960s called *Magilla Gorilla*. It was about a fun-loving primate and the pet shop where he spent his days causing trouble for the shop owner. I was a big fan growing up.

"Oh my goodness, *Magilla Gorilla!*" I cried. "You're watching *Magilla Gorilla*. That's my favorite cartoon. I used to watch it all the time as a kid."

The attendant turned and looked at me. It was the first time I actually saw him face-on. I wasn't sure what to expect when all of a sudden an enormous smile broke out on his face and giant laughter burst from within. It was such a huge reaction I felt like Magilla Gorilla himself was giggling at me.

"Oh, wow," Chris said deadpan from the passenger seat.

It was one of the most beautiful things I had witnessed in my life. As much as I wanted it to continue, there was a line of cars behind me waiting to exit, so I smiled at the attendant and pulled out of the garage.

The next day we pulled up to the gate, with Chris in the driver's seat. Guess what happened? Yep, the giant man looked up from his TV and noticed me. The big smile returned to his face.

"Hello," he said in a thick accent.

"Hello," I answered. "Have a nice day."

"Thank you," he said. It was obvious that his English wasn't very good, but he managed to add, "Have a nice day."

That was it. From that day forward, the attendant always greeted us with a big smile, and we pulled out into the rush-hour traffic feeling that much better for it.

Maybe you're waiting to hear that the man and I became friends, started meeting for breakfast once a week, and now he owns a bunch of parking garages around town. Nope. Nothing like that. But that was never the point.

It was just about making a meaningful connection. Because I was living with my eyes up, I had perceived the glimmer of goodness in this man. All I wanted was to bring it to the surface. It took months of persistence, but with *Magilla Gorilla* providing the much-needed spark, I was able to make a human connection. And we both benefited from it.

⊙⊙ TJ's Takeaway

Every day brings an opportunity to connect with someone new. When we make an effort to engage, whether with a friendly smile, an encouraging nod, or an inquisitive prod, this is the magic, the spark where authentic and meaningful connections begin. But the spark doesn't always come with the first strike, as the story about the parking garage attendant shows. Here's where persistence comes in, the all-important fifth P. To be a truly transformative person, you often have to work hard to make others around you go from invisible to visible. It's about being intentional and seeing who in your universe could use a lift, then going out and making the connection. It's often been my experience that just when you're ready to give up, the spark will light.

Turning the Mentorship Model on Its Head

Traditional mentoring has always been a top-down model. The older, wiser boss or manager takes the young hire under their wing, filling him or her with all the wisdom of their years. This is how you close a deal, the seasoned sales director will say. This is how you handle the patient, the veteran doctor will instruct. This is how you deal with an unruly student, the tenured teacher will advise.

There's nothing inherently wrong with top-down mentoring; wisdom certainly comes from experience as most of us have benefited from it, but in my experience this model leans toward the transactional. In exchange for the guidance and direction, the mentee pledges loyalty to their mentor. It's a way to keep the hierarchy of an organization intact.

As you might guess, I'm not a huge fan of hierarchies. That's why I've always preferred side-to-side or even bottom-up mentoring. Through decades of coaching, I have learned as much from my players as I've taught them (think about Muji's selflessness in chapter nine or Bert's search for meaning in chapter ten). These relationships have been truly transformational on both sides.

This perspective on mentoring was shaped by my first official coaching job when I was nineteen years old, back in the summer of '79, shortly after I started the soccer club in my community. One day, I was busy picking up cones after a camp session, when a guy approached me from the parking lot. He was built like a fireplug, with a shiny head and a wad of chewing tobacco lodged in his cheek.

"Looks like you know your way around a soccer field," he said jovially, then stuck out his hand. "Bob Knowles, good to meet you."

"TJ Kostecky," I said. "Likewise."

"I'm the director of athletics at Jefferson High," Bob continued. "We've been winning enough championships in football and baseball, and now I'm looking for a new soccer coach to do the same thing."

"Is that right?" I said, vaguely paying attention.

"Here's the thing," Bob said. "I wouldn't know a corner kick from a kick in the pants. I need someone to help me build the team. Interested?"

That's how I landed my first coaching position, as the assistant for Jefferson High's varsity soccer team. Boy, were we awful. I'll never forget our first practice. I started the team out with a basic shooting drill with overlapping runs, but it was too advanced. So

I showed them how to shoot. Balls went flying in every direction. Next, I tried a simple passing drill, just distributing the ball back and forth. It was too advanced. "This should be interesting," I said to Bob, the two of us watching from the sideline.

"I have total faith in you," he said with a smile and a clap on my shoulder.

I'm not sure we scored a single goal that season, let alone won a game. And yet, it was such a positive experience, largely because Bob did have so much belief in me. He saw the coach that I would become. He permitted me to make mistakes, which I eventually learned from, and empowered me to realize my potential. I ended up staying on as his assistant for the next seven years as we eventually turned the program into a winner.

You might be thinking to yourself, this sounds like a pretty top-down mentorship—and it's true, Bob did impart so many valuable lessons to me in that time, including how to get over my fear of public speaking. Though I now make my living addressing large audiences, I used to be terrified of speaking in public, unless it was a group of kids in shin guards huddled on a grass field. Bob eased me into it. That first year, at our end-of-year dinner, he had me up on the stage with him, handing out awards. The next season, I read off the player names, nervously shaking as my voice cracked. The season after that, I said a few more words about each player. By year four, I was emceeing the ceremony. Bob helped me find my voice, helped me build confidence in myself, and I haven't looked back since.

So yes, there was an element of top-down mentoring to the relationship. But Bob was also wholly receptive to what I had to teach him about soccer. Being twenty years my senior and an experienced, accomplished coach, albeit in a different sport, he could have easily had a chip on his shoulder. Instead, he was able to check his ego, show real vulnerability, and accept the help I had to offer.

I checked in with Bob during the writing of this book. Some four decades had passed since we first joined forces on the field of Jefferson High. We'd kept in touch over the years, so I was eager to hear how the experience of us coaching together sat in his memory.

"As an American football coach with twenty-seven years of playing and coaching experience, it was safe to say that I was not a big fan of soccer," he said over the phone. "I couldn't appreciate a sport where you weren't permitted to use your hands. It seemed dumb to me."

"That was pretty obvious at first." I laughed.

"But then you had so much passion and excitement for the game that my own perspective started to shift," he continued. "You were still in college, but you were an innovator who had the uncanny ability to break down the details of the game and make it understandable and fun for our players and for me. Your enthusiasm was contagious and spread throughout Jefferson Township."

"Coach, that really means a lot," I told him, "especially given how much you did for me in that time. In just two years, we doubled the interest in the sport, taking it from two teams of seventeen players to three teams of twenty-two each. That was huge at the time."

"It was. But the biggest takeaway for this American football coach was embracing and falling in love with the beautiful game as I continued to stay on and coach long after you moved on. These were some of the most exciting years of my life."

👓 TJ's Takeaway

The traditional mentorship model is a one-way street, with all the wisdom moving from old to young. It misses out on so many opportunities for learning and growth. The key to making these relationships more mutually beneficial is vulnerability. It's about letting go of the idea that you have to know everything and be in charge at all times, the way Coach Knowles did with me all those years ago. His willingness to check his ego enabled him to widen his lens and take in the beauty of soccer. He didn't give up anything in the process, and in fact his standing in the community only grew. As you move through life, constantly applying the first P, perception, look for learning and inspiration from everyone around you, not just those who seem to be ahead in the game.

A Late-Night Call from a Onetime Nemesis

It was after midnight on a frigid February night in 2015 when my phone started buzzing on my bedside table. You always think the worst with unexpected late-night calls, so I was relieved when the name on the screen wasn't a close family member or friend. Instead, it was probably the last person in a million years I thought would be calling: Shaun Green.

For the better part of two decades, Shaun and I had been rival coaches in the Northeast Conference—me at LIU and Shaun at Central Connecticut State University, where he ran the program from 1984 to 2019. To say it was a bitter rivalry would be an understatement. I'm not gonna lie—I couldn't stand the guy, with his brash attitude and win-at-any-cost approach to the game. And he thought even less of me. I recall one match in 1999 when the sideline sparring between the two of us nearly came to physical blows. It was not my finest moment, as I allowed Shaun to bring this out in me.

Here he was calling after midnight in the middle of the offseason. I thought about letting it go to voicemail, but the stronger voice in my head told me to pick up the phone.

"Shaun . . ." I said, trying to sound as nonchalant as possible.

"Hey, TJ, how are you, mate?" Shaun said in his distinctive Newcastle English accent. It was obvious from the slurring of words that he'd had a few.

"I'm doing okay," I said evenly, still trying to sound as if there was nothing at all unusual about the timing of the call. My Five Ps were fully awake and I sensed from the start that all was not right in the life of Shaun Green. "How are you doing, Shaun?" I asked.

"Not so well," he answered, confirming my hunch.

Shaun then proceeded to share with me the many ways that his personal life had gone off the rails in recent months, starting with the breakup of his marriage of thirty-seven years. Other relationships in his life were suffering as a result and he had lost his way. It was perhaps the lowest point in his life. All the bravado had been beaten out of him and he basically went from being a jerk to a raw, vulnerable, humble guy.

My first instinct was to go into empathy mode, so I started by relating the struggles I endured with my own divorce.

"There were some very dark nights of the soul during that time," I said. "But I came out the other side so much stronger and happier. You will too."

Shaun heard me, but I could tell the words weren't going through. Sometimes it's not enough to hear how others have been in your shoes before. It's easy to tell yourself that their situation couldn't possibly be as bad as what you're experiencing. This was the mindset that Shaun was locked in.

I decided to take another tack and remind him of all the good that was in him. As I think I've made it clear, I was not president of the Shaun Green Fan Club at the time. But as my perception of the situation kicked in, I was able to check any feelings of judgment and come at Shaun with a wide, open lens. I was able to find the good in him.

I reminded him of the challenges he had faced in the past and how his ability to overcome them modeled positive behavior for his players, as well as his own children. In one legendary incident, Shaun had suffered a massive heart attack that landed him in the hospital. He checked himself out of the hospital early so that he could be on the sideline to coach his team right here in Brooklyn.

"That might not have been the smartest decision for your health," I joked, "but the passion and commitment it showed your players will be with them forever."

The conversation went on like this for the next hour. It bounced around from soccer to family to the highs and lows and stresses of coaching at the Division I level for decades. At every turn, I reminded Shaun of the good in him. By the end of the call, the cloud had lifted.

"This is going to change your life for the better," I said, in closing.

"Thank you, TJ," he answered, and we hung up.

Seven months later, I had another call from Shaun, this time in the middle of the morning.

"TJ, my life is flipped," he said. "I met a wonderful woman, I'm controlling the things I can control, and I'm in such a better place as a result."

A year or so later, Shaun had me as a guest on *SoccerCoachTV*, his show on YouTube that's grown into one of the most watched coaching platforms in the world, with more than twenty-five million views. I thought we were going to talk about soccer, and there was plenty of that. But Shaun opened the segment by recounting our midnight call.

"TJ and I have become very close friends," he started. "When I was going through a tough time in my life, dealing with a lot of personal challenges, I was home one night alone, drunk as a skunk. I reached out to TJ even though we'd never really had an intimate relationship. He took my call and we chatted and we've become really tight brothers since then. He really helped me, and on the show today I think you'll see why."

That's one of the nicest intros I've ever received and definitely the one that means the most to me. I was thankful that he had reached out to me that evening and happy I took Shaun's call in his hour of need.

TJ's Takeaway

The good in others isn't always staring you in the face. It can be hidden by any number of things, including miscommunications and false judgments. This is why it's so important to refresh your lens and be willing to see people and situations in a different light. By all means, trust your gut and steer clear of people who are truly toxic. But if there's the benefit of the doubt, give the good a chance to shine through by keeping your lens as wide, deep, and bright as possible. And remember the power of kindness. I'll end with a quote from one of my go-to gratitude guides, *The 1325 Buddhist Ways to Be Happy*: "One compassionate word, action, or thought can reduce a person's suffering and bring that person joy . . . One action can save a person's life . . . One thought can do the same, because thoughts always lead to words and actions."

A Daughter in Distress

When my daughter Kate was twenty-four, she pursued the dream of many twentysomethings by moving to New York City. At first, it was the life she imagined—living in a brownstone on the Upper East Side, walking to work each morning along Central Park to her gleaming glass office on the fortieth floor of Rockefeller Plaza, taking Pilates classes at her cushy gym with other bright, young professionals.

But after a few months, the sheen of city life started to dim, its place taken by a nagging loneliness and feelings of anxiety. As she told me over the phone one night, "This life might be a dream, but it's not my dream." I did what most dads in that situation would do and encouraged her to give it a little more time.

"Transitions are always hard, and this is a major one you've undertaken," I said. "Let's see how you're feeling after a few more weeks."

Knowing what I do now, I would have chosen my words differently. But I truly believed Kate would find her way. She's always been fiercely independent and capable of anything she puts her mind to. I remember on a whim Donna and I gave her a unicycle for her twelfth birthday. In spite of numerous falls, she persisted and went on to master it in a few short weeks.

As I would soon learn, though, this challenge was greater than any she'd faced. Her anxiety continued to spike, along with her disillusionment with New York. She hated the cold (both the weather and the temperament of many New Yorkers) and fantasized about living somewhere warm, within walking distance of the ocean. She even filled her apartment with prints of palm trees and the sea, but it was little comfort.

As her anxiety grew, so did her insomnia, to the point where she was going days and days without sleep. She tried to find a doctor to see her, only to be told the wait time was as much as four months.

One night, in need of a distraction, she decided to join a friend for an Indie rock concert at a downtown venue. The stimulation sent her into a full-blown panic attack, complete with an out-of-body experience where she was looking down at herself from above. She told her friend she needed to get some air and made a beeline for the exit.

As soon as she reached the sidewalk, she called me. I was living in Brooklyn at the time, but unfortunately, I was visiting family in upstate New York. The fear in Kate's voice poured through the phone line.

"Can you get back to your apartment safely?" I asked her.

"Yes," she said.

"Good," I responded. "I'll be there in five hours."

"I don't think I can go to work tomorrow," she said.

"Don't," I told her. "For the first time in your life, call in sick. I'll be there when you wake up and we'll figure this out together."

Finding the good with loved ones takes on a different dynamic. Especially with your own child, you're naturally inclined to see the best. So the process is more about holding space for them so that they can find the good in themselves. This was the approach I took with Kate, starting that first morning. It was obvious that her unhappiness at work was as much a part of her malaise as her disenchantment with New York City.

"But if I quit my job, I'll never be hired again," Kate said, sipping nervously from a cup of hot tea.

"That's just not true," I responded. "You earned a degree from an incredible school, you have an amazing resume, and your colleagues love working with you. Anyone would be thrilled to hire you. You have to believe that."

I could see the skepticism on her face. So I made her an offer I knew she couldn't resist.

"Tell you what," I said. "If you put in your two weeks' notice tomorrow, you can join me on my upcoming trip to Greece, which is exactly fifteen days away."

She went for it. A couple weeks later, we were basking in the glow of one of the most enchanting places on earth, Athens. Travel of any kind is an excellent way to refresh your lens, but the impact is even greater when you're surrounded by the likes of the Parthenon and the Acropolis.

When we weren't visiting ancient ruins, we enjoyed Greece's more carefree side—laughter-filled lunches along the coast, people-watching over glasses of wine and ouzo, savoring the city's wonderful street food. One night, we were lounging at an outdoor bar after a long day of sightseeing, watching the world go by.

"This is what I want my life to look like," Kate said.

"What about it?" I asked, pushing for deeper meaning.

"I don't want to be rushed," Kate continued. "I want to be able to enjoy moments like this. I want to live somewhere where it's warm enough to sit outside in the evening. I want to be able to drive to the sea at a moment's notice. I want to connect with people who have the time to talk to me."

"Then make that your life," I said. "You are in control. You can design the life of your dreams."

Within a week of our return home, Kate flew to Savannah, Georgia, to interview for a new job. They put her up in a beautiful guesthouse built in the 1800s, with a wraparound porch overlooking a lush park. As she described to me over the phone that night, it was the golden hour when she arrived, with magical light streaming through the Spanish moss hanging from the massive oak trees lining the brick sidewalk.

She ditched her puffer jacket and enjoyed the early spring evening with a walk downtown for dinner. She made her way to a restaurant with outdoor seating, reminiscent of Athens, and found a spot at the bar. A couple dining next to her invited her to join their conversation. They even insisted she try some of the food they had ordered. After dinner, they all walked down to the Savannah riverfront before parting ways. It was warm and peaceful, and Kate was happy.

Needless to say, she accepted the position and has since built a life around sunshine, adventure, and meaningful connections. And she can jump in her purple pickup truck and drive to nearby Tybee Island whenever she needs a dip in the sea.

TJ's Takeaway

When finding the good in others—and helping them find it in themself—it's important to remember that our goals are constantly changing. That's true for groups, be it a soccer team or Fortune 500 company, and it's certainly true for individuals. Especially when working with someone who is still finding meaning and their place in the world, remind them that the one constant in life is change. Embrace the change. One of the biggest challenges we all face is being true to ourselves in a world that is trying to make us all the same. Remember the power of modeling: when you believe the moment is right, have the courage and audacity to go for it, to pursue your dream. It will inspire others to do the same.

The Unlikely Locker Room Leader

By the 2010s, the LIU Blackbirds had become a perennial DI powerhouse. Brooklyn had exploded, too, into a mecca of cool, driving big interest to the university. Put those two facts together and, absolutely no joke, I used to get five or more emails or calls a day from high school seniors who wanted to come play for us. If I'd given them all a shot, the number of attendees at our preseason tryouts would have been in the hundreds. Recruiting became exponentially easier.

That was the state of things when, one morning in the fall of

2015, I got a call from Gregorio Mount, an Italian-born midfielder who had spent most of his life living and playing in Seattle.

"Hello, Coach, my name is Gregorio and I would love to be a part of your 2016 roster at LIU," he said confidently.

I was impressed by his composure and self-assuredness. But his soccer resume and video? Not as much. After reviewing both, I knew we had prospects who were higher on our list. As we chatted more that morning, it was also clear that he had done his homework. He didn't just know about LIU's success, but also about the culture of the program we had created. He knew all about the coaching courses I taught, right down to the syllabi, and shared his interest in pursuing a career in soccer, even if it wasn't on the field. He had a self-awareness well beyond his years. Still, that didn't change the fact that he simply wasn't on the level soccer-wise.

"I need to be straight with you, Gregorio," I said as the call was winding down. "It's a very competitive roster and I don't see a spot for you. But let's keep in touch as you continue your search."

He thanked me for my time and we hung up. I thought that might be the last I'd ever hear of Gregorio Mount, but a few weeks later I received an email. He explained that he'd met with half a dozen other colleges, including some very good ones, like Lehigh, Lafayette, and Temple. Impressive though they were, he still believed he belonged at LIU.

"I know you don't see me on your team, but I want to be a part of it," he wrote. "I can see myself learning from the culture that you've built."

My first instinct as a soccer coach was to hold firm and keep Gregorio off the team. But the other voice in my head kept coming back to his persistence and authenticity, two qualities that are critical to Vision Training for Life. I was sure Gregorio would not be an impactful player on the field. But I was equally certain that he would impact the culture of the team by carrying forward our ethos. I decided to bring him on board.

As it turned out, both my instincts were right. Gregorio didn't see a lot of playing time over his four-year career. But he was an enormous contributor to our success during that time, including three trips to the conference championship.

One moment in particular stands out. Earlier in the book I mentioned a player from that era named Rasmus Hansen, our leading scorer and one of the best players to come through the program during my tenure. Like a lot of superstars, Rasmus could be a bit prickly, to put it mildly.

The team was in the conference room, going over the video after a rare loss. We were breaking down a goal the other team scored off a quick counterattack. Players and coaches were offering different analyses of the play, none of them hitting it on the head. From the very back of the room, Gregorio raised his hand.

"What do you see, Gregorio?" I asked.

"Well, if Rasmus had pressed their left back sooner, they never would have broken our midfield line with the quick outlet pass," he said.

The room went quiet. Here was one of our less heralded players on the squad calling out one of the best, in front of everyone. It wouldn't have surprised me at all if, in the next moment, Rasmus's chair went flying across the room. Instead, after an uncomfortable quiet pause, this happened.

"You're right, Gregorio," Rasmus said. "I need to press harder there."

The next match, Rasmus worked his tail off and netted a pair of goals in a win over our biggest conference rival.

About five years later, I received a call from a Major League Soccer executive. Gregorio had applied for a top job at the organization, working for the MLS Players Association, which is all about empowering the players by establishing a supportive community. Gregorio had listed me as his reference. I shared the story of Gregorio's ability to call out and inspire Rasmus, because he had established so much trust with his teammates through years of integrity, care, and authenticity.

"We thought Gregorio was the right person for the job," the MLS rep said. "That story confirms it."

⌕ TJ's Takeaway

The power of self-belief is one of, if not the most crucial indicators for lifetime success. Any time you can help instill it in others, you will lift them up for life. Keep your eyes wide open and never shut the door on someone who has the insatiable drive to be a part of your company or team. A teammate with passion, inspiration, and wisdom may very well be the catalyst that motivates others and contributes to your collective success. Remember—if you think you can or if you think you can't, you're right. Think you can!

The Best Little Bodega in Brooklyn

In the swath of downtown Brooklyn surrounding LIU, there's a bodega on just about every corner. From the outside, these small, family-owned grocers, selling everything from candy to canned goods, can all look the same. But get to know them better and you realize that every bodega is unique. Some trade in booze and cigarettes, others are all about the lottery, and others do brisk business around their deli counter (which bodega makes the best bacon, egg, and cheese is a hotly debated topic among New Yorkers).

When I first started at LIU in 1999, I tried out a dozen or more bodegas before claiming the one on the corner of Ashland Place and Dekalb Avenue as my own. It had a cheerful vibe, starting with the man behind the counter, Safir, who always greeted customers with a smile. It was a bustling scene, especially if you mistimed it and got caught in the swarm of students just let out from Brooklyn Tech, the massive high school located a couple blocks east.

I'd go in for a coffee and a buttered roll, or an afternoon snack, four or five times a week. Every now and then, the bodega would be closed at odd times of the day. I knew Safir and his crew were from Yemen, so I put two and two together and figured they were engaged in Muslim prayer. It was always a bummer seeing the "back in fifteen minutes" sign on the door, but I was tolerant of other cultures and religious customs.

At least I thought I was. A couple years into my time at LIU, 9/11 happened. I'll never forget the throngs of people walking over the Manhattan and Brooklyn Bridges, streaming down Flatbush Avenue to points south, including the farthest corners of the borough.

The ensuing backlash against the Muslim community was real. Though I remained tolerant, I realize in hindsight that the sense of otherness I felt toward Muslims intensified after 9/11. I still went to the bodega and traded greetings with Safir, but more than ever it felt like there was a cultural divide between us.

It stayed that way for many years. Then one night I happened to be in a different bodega closer to my home in another part of Brooklyn. I'd been out to dinner with a recruit and his family and craved something sweet after the meal. The guys at this bodega were particularly friendly, so we chatted for a few minutes while I made my purchase.

It turned out they were from Yemen. My mind went to Safir, and a moment from a few weeks prior. He hadn't been around for several months, so I asked his fill-in behind the counter where he was.

"Back home in Yemen," he answered.

"What's he doing there?" I asked.

"Family," the man said. "His wife and children are in Yemen. He goes back to take care of them. Many other relatives too."

Later that night, for the first time in my life, I went online and read about Yemen. I learned that it was the scene of one of the worst humanitarian crises in the world, with more than 80 percent of the population living below the poverty line. Millions of Yemeni were (and still are) stuck in makeshift refugee camps. Food insecurity rates were off the charts, as were the number of people without safe drinking water.

I recalled all of this as I paid for my KitKat and bantered with the Yemeni cashier and cook behind the counter. Then I had a thought.

"Hey, could you teach me a few words of Arabic?" I asked.

"Sure, why not?" they said.

"Okay, how do you say 'How are you?'" I asked.

"Kayfa haluka," they said. I repeated the words back until I got the pronunciation right.

"And how do you say 'Thank you'?"

"Shukran lak."

"What about 'God be with you'?"

"Allah maaka," they instructed.

I thanked them for the impromptu Arabic lesson and exited the bodega, repeating the words in my head the whole way home. A few weeks later, I popped into my regular bodega for breakfast and was happy to see Safir manning the register. As the deli guy prepared my order, I turned to Safir.

"Safir, kayfa haluka?" I asked.

"Coach, you speak Arabic!" he cried, his eyes radiating light.

"Just a few words," I answered.

The deli guy handed me my buttered roll.

"Shukran lak," I said. He was all smiles too.

"Listen to that!" Safir said with a laugh, as I paid for my order. "You are like a true Yemeni."

"Allah maaka, my friend," I said and made my way out of the bodega.

From that day forward, Safir wouldn't let me pay for anything. He'd literally push my money back into my hands. It got to a point where I had to quickly drop my cash on the counter and run out of the store.

That's how much Safir appreciated the simple connection that occurred between us when I made the decision to learn a few words from his language. A spark was lit and it made the bodega an even warmer, brighter space that I looked forward to being in every single day. And on those rare occasions when Safir and the crew were praying and the store was closed, I'd hold off on the afternoon coffee or snack. This was my bodega. I would wait for its doors to open again.

👓 TJ's Takeaway

To find the good in others, oftentimes we first have to find, or expand, the good in ourselves. Especially in the wake of 9/11, I allowed my preconceived notions of Muslims to narrow my lens on the community. As a result, I couldn't see the incredible sacrifice and generosity that Safir was making for his family back in Yemen. Instead of finding common points between us, I was focused on the differences. Once I refreshed my lens, I could set aside my biases and form a connection with Safir that brought deeper joy and meaning to our daily interactions. I always knew that Safir was a good man. I now realized he was a great one.

Chapter Thirteen

CONCLUSION

So that's my story. To wrap things up, I want to start by thanking you for giving me the chance to share it with you. Just as there are no coaches without players, no priests without congregations, and no doctors without patients, there are no storytellers without an audience to take in the narrative. Regardless of whether you and I ever meet face-to-face (and I hope very much that we do), our stories are now intertwined through the connection that forms between every author and their readers. I am grateful for that and I am grateful for you.

This story opened a couple hundred pages ago with the life-altering eye injury that I endured at the age of twelve. It was a seminal moment for me, no doubt. But the process of writing this book has made it clear how much my journey, like anyone's, is not about any one single moment, but rather the collection of experiences that weave together to form the tapestry of life. To draw a more fitting analogy, a ninety-minute soccer match can never be reduced to a single play. Sure, there are tight contests where a stroke of genius by one player leads to the deciding goal. But even in that example, a series of events had to occur to make the moment possible. Maybe it was the ball played three passes earlier that helped unlock the defense. Or the decoy run that pulled the keeper just enough out of position. Or some random play from years earlier that the goal scorer recalled and then used to execute the perfect placement of his shot.

This is how life unfolds. Every day, all around us, there are connections waiting to happen, discoveries waiting to be made, talents waiting to be unleashed—but only to those who move through life with their lens wide, bright, and deep, ready and willing to seize upon the moment. Remember my instruction to every new player who I have the opportunity to coach: Go out there and give me five looks every ten seconds. This one simple change to their game, this one shift in perspective, unleashes so much potential. Their game gets better from day one.

That's my challenge to you. Go out there today and get five more looks than you otherwise would, using the tools I've talked about throughout this book. Engage with the person at the checkout counter. Give extra thanks for something that happened this week. Identify a new goal for yourself and come up with a plan for achieving it. These are not major tasks. I'm not telling you to find a cure for cancer. I only want you to make subtle shifts in perspective to open up your field of vision and help you see more opportunities to connect with the people around you. It's through intentional connections that we thrive. It's through meaningful connections that our universe expands. I believe you can do it. I believe we can do it together. What do you say? Let's lift our **eyes up**, score big in the game of life, and make this world a better place.

Acknowledgments

O ne of my biggest worries is that I might have forgotten someone here. Please forgive me in advance if I left you out.

But one person that I am forever grateful to is Dan DiClerico. A visionary and world-class writer, who saw events from my collective experience that he imagined would enrich your lives. Dan had exceptional skills and shined a steady light on my story that made it land. I'm thankful for your guidance, patience, persistence, and friendship.

Eternally thankful to Len Bilous, the wise sage who's gotten me to look at the beautiful game through a rich, expansive lens. Not many folks are fortunate enough to have their own personal Yoda as I do.

And thanks to Stephen (Hoogie) Hoogerwerf for insisting that Dan and I connect over coffee, thinking we may have something in common. Boy, were you right!

A shout-out to the fabulous folks at Matt Holt Books: First, Matt Holt, who entrusted us with this project and whose friendship and generosity I'm grateful for. Thank you to Katie Dickman for your diligent and inspiring editorial advice, and to Brigid Pearson for your clever and eye-catching jacket design. A big thank-you as well to Kerri Stebbins and Mallory Hyde for your insight, effort, and wisdom steering the all-important marketing campaign.

All my thanks to the incomparable Lisa Gallagher, our literary agent, for holding my hand throughout the last two years and walking me through a maze of uncharted waters. And thanks to Joe Barcia for your detailed research that supports the lessons throughout the book.

From the bottom of my heart, thank you, George and Nadine Hayduchok, for being there for support and to lift me up when I need it, for your incisive feedback on our early drafts, and for modeling the best parental behavior on the planet. Whenever your ears begin to ring, you can thank me as I keep singing your praises.

A special shout-out to my all-important mentors: Bob Knowles, Norman Schwartz, Mal Simon, Roachel Laney, John Suarez, Margaret Alaimo, Bob Reasso, Gene Spatz, and David Lindholm. Your wisdom, patience, courage, integrity, and standard of excellence are qualities that I've admired and strive to embrace in my own life. Above all, thank you for believing in me.

For their generosity, love, and support at different stages of this project, I must thank my mom, Lucy Hryniszak; sister, Nina Lauria; cousins Len and Leon Hayduchok, and Nina Hall and Ludmilla Lucheck; nieces Danielle Pomper, Laura Hayduchok, Anastasia Lauria Nasuta, and Maria Lauria; nephew, Willie Lauria; and son-in-law, Dan Brown.

And my endless gratitude to Don Maggi, Vic Furmanec, Chris

Innvar, David (Mac) MacMillan, Jim (Step) Stepahin, Mike Buday, Joe Borrino, Glenn Crooks, JR Hann, Evan Weller, Scott Yerger, David Sisson, Alex Elias, Jeroen Hofstede, Chris Lawrence, Eric Masters, Bernie Hernando III, Nate Bell, Brad Johnson, Jonas Stigh, Mustapha (Moose) Ayoub, Gregorio Mount, Jukka Lehto, Andrew Zarick, Ricardo Alexander M. Ordain, Ryan Vanderkin, Brice Merwine, Matt Harmer, Robert (Bert) Black, Paul Stahlschmidt, Bryan Cunningham, Matt Harmer, Tim Rands, Karen and Ken Wright, Michelle and Lucas Parin, Dominic Casciato, Sam Sabaliauskas, Wim Rijsbergen, Kari Raita, Oliver Smith, Daniel Solis, Jose Rodriques, Malia Du Mont, Craig Thorpe-Clark, Paul Marienthal, John Michael (JM) Richards, Paul LaBarbera, Leo and Kate Marianiello, Krista and David Neu, Caroline Des Posada, Jimmy Rodewald, Jim Sheahan, Dr. Joe Machnik, Dr. Tracy Trevorrow, Adam Janssen, Robin Graham, Dan Blank, Michael Minogue, Terry Wansart, Simon Clements, Shaun Green, Roman Ponos, Dr. George Pappas, and Lee Taylor. For those of you I missed, please know that it's not you, it's me.

To all of my assistants and former players, you know who you are. Four decades of our collective experiences serve as the foundation for this book. You've taught me the importance of being patient, empathetic, resilient, and present. Thanks for enriching my life. I appreciate all of you.

Kate and Caroline, properly thanking you would take a whole other book. I love you to the moon and back!

Selected Bibliography

Chapter Two

Chris Anderson and David Sally, *The Numbers Game: Why Every-thing You Know About Soccer Is Wrong* (Penguin Books, 2013).

Chapter Four

Ben Lyttleton, *Edge: What Business Can Learn from Football* (Harper-Collins, 2017).
Mihaly Csikszentmihalyi and Susan Jackson, *Flow in Sports: The Keys to Optimal Experiences and Performances* (Human Kinetics, 1999).

Chapter Five

Shawn Achor, *The Happiness Advantage* (Currency, 2010).
Paul Ehrlich and Robert Ornstein, *Humanity on a Tightrope: Thoughts*

on Empathy, Family, and Big Changes for a Viable Future (Rowman & Littlefield Publishers, 2012).

Sebastian Abbot, *The Away Game: The Epic Search for Soccer's Next Superstars* (W. W. Norton & Company, 2018).

Chapter Six

Martin Seligman, "Empirical Validation of Interventions," *American Psychologist*, 2005.

Robert Emmons, "10 Ways to Become More Grateful," *Greater Good Magazine*, 2010.

Bernard Beitman, *Connecting with Coincidence, The New Science for Using Synchronicity and Serendipity in Your Life* (Health Communications Inc, 2016).

Margaret Shih, *Stereotype Susceptibility: Identity Salience and Shifts in Quantitative Performance* (Psychological Science, 1999).

Chapter Seven

San Diego Loyal, Twitter post, October 1, 2020, 2:27 AM, https://twitter.com/SanDiegoLoyal/status/1311553192711184385.

"Let the Kids Play," YouTube video, 1:00, posted by Major League Baseball, October 2, 2018, https://www.youtube.com/watch?v=VZfEv4JqxHQ.

Chapter Eight

Alex Wood and Deepak Chopra, "The Role of Gratitude in Spiritual Well-Being in Asymptomatic Heart Failure Patients," *American Psychological Association*, 2015.

Lynn Novick, *College Behind Bars* (PBS, 2019).

Sara Weissman, "Education Behind and Beyond Bars" (Inside Higher Ed, 2019).

Chapter Nine

Katrien Fransen, *The Competence-Supportive and Competence-Thwarting Role of Athlete Leaders: An Experimental Test in a Soccer Context* (Public Library of Science, 2018).

Addie J. Bracy, *Mental Training for Ulrarunning* (Human Kinetics, 2022).

Chapter Ten

Viktor Frankl, *Man's Search for Meaning* (Beacon Press, 1946).

About the Authors

TJ Kostecky has coached thousands of players and coaches around the world over the past forty years. He is the lead innovator of Vision Training, a developmental program that empowers athletes to maximize their playing potential. Through his myriad experiences, Kostecky realized that widening your vision has the power to transform not only how players approach their sport, but also how they approach life.

TJ is now at Bard College (Annondale-On-Hudson, NY), where he conducts leadership training workshops for the college deans, various administration staffs, citizen science fellows, and student groups, in addition to running the men's soccer program. Previously, he spent twenty years at Long Island University-Brooklyn, teaching in the Department of Sports Science, cofounding the university's

Sport Management Program, and serving as the Men's Division I soccer coach.

Worldwide, TJ conducts Vision Training seminars and transformational leadership workshops for organizations, sports teams, coaches, parents, and players. He co-produced the #1 bestselling Vision Training Soccer on the Attack video and complementary coaches' manual. TJ continues to teach players and coaches an innovative training method, which empowers them to make their own decisions, gain confidence, and become creative in their play. His travels have taken him to places such as Finland, Guatemala, Iceland, Norway, Ukraine, Costa Rica, Jamaica, Canada, and Turks and Caicos. In 2020, he was inducted into the Ukrainian Sports Hall of Fame.

He is the proud father of two young women: Kate Brown and Caroline Kostecky, both assistant admission directors at the Savannah College of Art and Design. TJ resides in Tivoli, New York, where his play involves longboarding throughout the village streets, hiking the Catskill Mountains, and engaging everyone in conversation.

Dan DiClerico is an award-winning journalist, a memoirist, and a biographer who specializes in motivational, inspirational, and business books, as well as wellness, sports, and lifestyle. A lifelong soccer player, coach, and fan, he can often be found on the pitches of Brooklyn, New York, the borough where he lives with his wife and kids.

More Ways to Connect with TJ

Take the next step on your leadership journey with TJ Kostecky's insightful eTraining course, "Transformative Leadership." Expanding on the key lessons of *Eyes Up!*, Kostecky offers practical strategies to elevate your leadership skills in sports and life.

As a special offer, readers can unlock an exclusive discount using code EYESUP at checkout. Scan the QR code (left) now to begin your leadership transformation.

Interested in learning more about Vision Training for Soccer? Enroll in our online Level 1 course today and learn how to teach players to scan the field and communicate visually. Scan the QR code (left) or visit www.visiontrainingsoccer.com.

 Interested in connecting with TJ? His interactive, ninety-minute workshops engage participants as they discover specific ways to become effective leaders and lead more meaningful lives. Scan the QR code (left) or visit www.visiontrainingforlife.com today to learn more.